CW00408731

Selling Without Shaking Hands

How To Sell From Anywhere

By Glenn Blackman
& Mike Vince

ISBN: 979-8-6823-9468-5

CONTENTS

Introduction - You Cannot Sell In The Same Way Anymore

The coronavirus pandemic has changed the world forever, rapidly accelerating the adoption of technology to eliminate, or at least minimise, face-to-face (F2F) contact. This was an effort to reduce the spread of the deadly virus, but even pre-pandemic much of what we might have called traditional F2F selling had begun to migrate away from the physical world, into the virtual world, through the adoption of technology.

The UK has been through a period of lockdown, where businesses were compelled to close, and people were prevented from having F2F contact with others. As the restrictions were eased so some F2F contact was reintroduced, however certain boundaries about personal contact remain. Commentators suggest that repeated bouts of social distancing could continue to be needed in the future, perhaps on a localised basis. However, history suggests that this will not be the last pandemic that we will experience, and so there is also a need to prepare to be able to cope with the possibility of future constraints, not to mention the attraction of the ongoing use of the technology that has helped us communicate throughout the current crisis. These influences have been driving us away from F2F contact and challenging how we have sold to customers in the past.

These changes have meant that the time-honoured tradition of shaking hands to "seal the deal", has disappeared, maybe forever. In part that change was being driven by efficiency. For example, it is far cheaper, and quicker, to enable buying over the internet, rather than to staff and pay for a physical shop. It is more efficient to phone a prospective customer, than to drive to see them. Purchasing has become more web based as buyers have become more relaxed and familiar with the security of the technology that enables them to buy over the internet. The pandemic has catalysed a change that was already happening – we have moved towards methods of communication with customers that make better use of the internet and other non F2F channels.

This book is all about "selling", which we define as "persuading someone to purchase". That gives us an extremely broad remit to include those that call themselves "salespeople", business owners that sell to customers, and even people that supply products over the internet without any direct contact with customers. Whenever you want to persuade someone to purchase, this book has something to help you become more effective.

For those that are involved with any type of sales activity times have changed, where you might have been able to jump in your car and meet customers F2F, that might not be so simple, desirable, or even possible. Much of the old way of selling was based on making friends with customers, and activity we refer to as "relationship building" throughout this book. From small children we are taught how to make friends. We then continue to develop and use those skills into adulthood.

It is easy to sell to someone if you can make them like you, and many people rely primarily on that skill to gain new customers. It is a skill that can be severely curtailed when you are unable to communicate F2F, in person.

These changes have given rise to a new challenge, the need to adapt our sales skills to sales processes to embrace the new world, truly utilising the communication channels that are now available to us. This calls for a different type of selling, one where we can no longer rely upon our old "tried and tested" methods. A new method is required, one that is based on more than just relationship building. We need a sales system that incorporates a deeper understanding of the dynamics of any sales situation so that we can adapt to this changed world.

We have called this book "Selling Without Shaking Hands", SWOSH for short as the gesture of shaking hands is offered as a symbolism for the old way of selling. This book is about how you can capitalise on the opportunity to successfully sell to customers from anywhere in the world.

About The Authors And How This Book Is Written

SWOSH has been jointly written by Glenn Blackman and Mike Vince. We had to come up with a way of identifying who was "speaking" at any given time, so we have used a simple approach. Whenever Mike speaks, the text is shown in *italics* – anything not in italics is Glenn.

Where we have extra material and anecdotes to offer, that might interrupt the flow of the book, we have placed them at the back, in the notes section with a superscript reference in the text.

When I studied for my MBA, the first thing we were taught was that any book should be read in the context of the person that had written it. To that end, I would like to give some background to the authors of this book.

Our Backgrounds

Mike and I have worked together for many years, in various roles. We first met whilst we both worked for a subsidiary of a high street bank. One of the great things about working for a bank is that they can provide you with a first-class business education. I was lucky enough to attend numerous training courses about all aspects of negotiation and the psychology of motivation, which formed the focus of my MBA.

At the time Mike was working on a large organisational change project, which I joined as a project manager. Mike left the bank to join a small independent invoice finance company as Sales Director.[i]

I continued within the bank's subsidiary, managing its marketing and product development, before leaving to set up my own business as a business strategy and marketing consultant. This involved selling my services to lots of different customers. We worked together again to recruit and develop Mike's sales team, and I diversified into phone-based marketing and research services, to feed his team with new enquiries.

As I again diversified my business interests to offer business finance brokerage services, we continued to work together as Mike had moved to a new role as the Managing Director of another business finance company, again we were able to recruit and introduce new customers to his sales team. Mike has since set up his own business offering his customers the benefit of his extensive experience in sales, sales training, and sales management.

Why We Wrote This Book

In the process of helping Mike with the strategic planning for his new business, we had spoken at length about all the sales techniques and know-how, that we had both acquired over many decades. We wanted to codify what we both have learned into a selling system, one that could be passed onto others.

The UK lockdown, due to the coronavirus pandemic, created a unique opportunity for us to take the time to write it all down. We also wanted to adapt our thinking to selling in the post-pandemic environment. Mike's extensive sales experience, and engaging communication style complements my more technical approach, we thought that the combination would produce the perfect blend. So that is what you are reading, a summary of both our "sales playbooks" - you are getting two for the price of one!

You will also find checkpoint summaries throughout, and a distillation of everything at the end, so you can skip straight to those if you don't want to read the detail.

Checkpoint Summary

1) The pandemic has changed how we interact with other people and hence how we sell.

2) A deeper understanding of the dynamics of selling is required to adapt and succeed.

Shaking Hands To Seal The Deal

This is a sales improvement book. It is about moving away from outdated habits towards something new. A better understanding of the dynamics that underpin the sales process, so that you can improve your effectiveness. We will illustrate our system in terms of a "sales balance" that is used to represent the dynamics of any sales situation. The balance tips towards, or away from a sale according to the weights that sit on each side of the balance. Once the tipping point is reached, the right-hand side of the balance moves downward, and the sale is achieved.

The following diagram is a simple visual representation of that:

THE SALES BALANCE

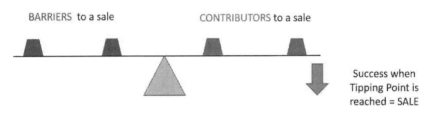

This deeper understanding of the mechanics of selling can yield benefits in situations where you cannot operate as you always have. If you understand how selling really works, and the psychology that determines how customers can be influenced to make decisions, you can apply that understanding to any situation. It does not matter if you can no longer get F2F with a customer, you can still use our approach to improve your effectiveness. Our methodology is about more than just acquiring sales skills, it is also about using all the channels that are at your disposal, to maximise your chances of success. Working smarter, rather than working harder.

A lot has changed within the sales process due to the lockdown restrictions, their gradual lifting, residual impacts, and the underlying adoption of new technology. Our symbolism for all this change is that the handshake, the epitome of concluding a deal in a F2F negotiation, which may have disappeared forever. To understand where we are going, we need at least a rudimentary understanding of where we have been. Therefore, the next section looks at the history of shaking hands.

Where It Began

Historians generally agree the handshake evolved to mean an agreement between parties who didn't speak the same language: a weaponless gesture that is both a peaceful greeting and one that signals mutual consent. As trading civilisations spread throughout the world, it's considered likely they shook hands with one another to serve both purposes. I have found no references to this action meaning aggression or distrust and studies of many civilizations show the handshake as a positive ritual.

Most people are right-handed, and the right hand would be where one would most likely hold their weapon. Therefore, by shaking hands with your right hands, both parties can see that neither party holds a weapon – it is a symbol of trust. It has grown to become a symbol of binding a deal between two parties, "shaking hands on it", a physical manifestation of a verbal contract (which is legally binding under UK law) between parties. One that often precedes a written contract, something that is demonstrably legally binding, that follows having reached that agreement.

Why It Is Important

Numerous psychological studies have shown that we live up to what we have signed up to. What might seem like a small change in behaviour, like signing an offer letter, can cause us to adhere to the outcome; to go through with our previous decision and not to back out later. We are more likely to stick to what we have agreed to when we put our name to it because we see this as a correct and proper way to behave. This also applies to a verbal commitment. Our language is peppered with phrases that show this to be true: "I'm a man of my word". Good salespeople are also taught to remind customers of a verbal contract when referencing a previous negotiation: "like we said".[ii]

But nothing beats the power of an agreement sealed with a handshake. In a world of sophisticated communication, we still use it to mean the same as our ancestors did.

So, it's no wonder you might feel concerned for the effectiveness of your sales outcomes when you can't greet people as you did and gain acceptance or agreement like you used to. Your instinct tells you that removal of such a powerful gesture will reduce your effectiveness. And that maybe true, but there is no avoiding it. In this book, we will explore what you can learn to do instead.

If we are unable to meet F2F, or even if we are only unable to shake hands on the deal when we do meet F2F, it may be superficially addressed by adding some alternative to the handshake. Perhaps you might go straight to getting a signature (even an electronic signature) on an order document, or even make light of the situation and suggest "shall we shake hands on that over the phone?".

However, there is much more scope to improve beyond just substituting a virtual alternative for a physical gesture. The real opportunity is to develop your sales skills to drive up your success rate, utilising a fundamental understanding of the dynamics of how sales occur, and how you can use all the communication channels that are available to set you up for ongoing success.

The Future Has Changed Forever

It's nothing new.

So, before you wring your hands and wonder how you will ever survive in sales in this new commercial reality, let me make you feel a little better. The world of selling without "touching" is not a new phenomenon. We have all shopped online. But there is a fundamental difference between what is bought and what is sold, and this book is about preparing you to do the latter differently and learning to do it better. We are dealing with crafting your message to influence decisions to buy from you. We will not focus upon the easy stuff where we all buy things because we want to and can afford to.

Although, many of the techniques set out in the book are equally applicable to selling products that people want and can afford. The underlying process, and purchasing psychology is the same.

That said, there is a lesson from the online shopping experience that we will reference later in this book: How to endorse the customer after they have chosen to buy from you. We do not want them to experience buyers' remorse, so they return the purchase or back out of the agreement.

Isn't it more that the rise of selling without meeting has just been bought into sharper focus? And that has caused companies, maybe your competitors, to respond by shortening their decision process. This has always happened in transactional based dealings that typically have a shorter lead time between "look at this" and "how much is it?". But it is now happening in relationship-based interactions, we have seen it in financial services. Data driven decision support mechanisms are not new either, but they are also on the rise.

Whist the shortening sales cycle presents some challenges, there are also efficiency gains to be had. It can even drive up conversion ratios. In the business finance sector, the "traditional" sales process was to receive an enquiry, dispatch your salesperson for an exploratory visit, issue an offer letter – perhaps after an initial credit committee meeting to approve the proposal. This was followed up with further due diligence visits and eventually a visit to bring the customer on board. Technology has enabled that process to be truncated. Approval "apps" have been developed that give the customer an immediate decision and pricing quote, without a visit, based on a few simple questions. You might argue that this loses the relationship building benefits of a visit, however it also has a few additional benefits to offer. Not only can a far larger volume of applications be handled but the customer is immediately seduced by the ease and speed of delivery. They may also be persuaded to think that if the application process is this straightforward, this will be a straightforward company to deal with. By comparison, competitors processes appear elongated and fraught with delays.

Taking away parts of our normal communication with others makes the sales process more difficult. During lockdown we were prevented from being able to meet F2F, and who knows when that restriction will raise its head once again. Another aspect of the lockdown has been where face masks are required to be worn, to prevent contagion. Whilst this may not be applicable all the time it deserves special mention as it makes even F2F communication particularly difficult. The issue is that most facial expression is covered which has a significant impact on your ability to judge someone's emotions and responses to what you are saying, let alone the impact it has on your voice.

When your communication processes are limited, you can only substitute a better understanding of the sales process and how to convert customers. You can no longer rely on what you have always done in the past.

So, what is the answer? Adaption to the new environment by improving your sales skills and a better understanding the selling process, you thereby improve your chances of converting more enquiries to purchases.

Speed Of Response

Adverts are riddled with the language of speed. "Sale must end Saturday", "Limited stock" "first come, first served", I am sure you have heard them all. You may even have used them. This appeals to our Fear Of Missing Out. But there is also another powerful force at play, especially for entrepreneurs.

And it means that a changed landscape of communication, particularly using "remote" meetings may not be so bad after all. You need to learn to recognise when to enhance the advantages of a swift offering, negotiation and close. To quickly illustrate:

A small business owner will often describe themselves as someone who is decisive, who acts quickly, who doesn't hesitate when they spot a gap in the market, a good deal, or an acquisition opportunity. Many will tell you it is an essential part of their success: because "snooze you lose". Their psychometric profiles would not usually include being data rational. They are not going to waste too much time on an in-depth analysis of endless figures or meetings. It is a gut feeling. It's their judgement. If they have a problem they usually want to "make it good and make it gone"

This means they often choose the first practical solution that emerges. In the US they call it "satisficing": a mash-up of being satisfactory and sufficient, that does the job. Yes, it's risky but it speaks to their image of themselves as a businessperson who gets what they want.

If your prospect is like this, you have an immensely powerful weight to tip the balance. Position your offering to deliver swiftly. Make sure the benefits can be delivered straight away.

This raises an important point about matching your processes and pace to the needs of your customer. If you sell to older people an internet-based offering may not be the best channel. If you sell to a younger demographic, internet may well be the best medium to engage with them – sending out paper-based leaflets could be seen as old fashioned.

Pace is a similar concern. Whilst you may want to achieve every sale in the fastest possible time, your customer may not always share your desire. To some extent you need to account for their needs, and match their pacing, however – the art is to keep the momentum moving at a rate that is at the upper levels that are within the range that your customer will accept.

Developing your Persuasion Proficiency

As we roll through this book, you will learn not to fear different channels of communication or those that you had not previously relied upon e.g. the phone call! We will show you how to foster the right circumstances that create and close sales opportunities in a shorter time than you did before. That doesn't mean cutting corners, its means recognising what will improve your conversion percentage. As you get more familiar with the idea of using the weights on the sales balance to help you, it will develop what we will call your "Persuasion Proficiency" (PP for short) and that means exactly what it sounds like.

There may also be opportunities for you to develop your approach to sales, to improve your PP. It is not just about adding tactics, skills, and techniques, it can also be improved by developing your sales process to encompass other media that you might not use at present. For example, do you keep in contact with prospective customers using a regular email update? You could add that to your process and, and a few additional sales may be rejuvenated and added to your pipeline. We have more on how to develop your processes to leverage all the available channels, later in the book.

Checkpoint Summary

1) You can no longer rely on what you have always done in the past.

2) Shaking hands on a deal is a symbol of how things used to be.

3) An increased speed of response is required to thrive in the new environment.

4) Your Persuasion Proficiency (PP) can be increased to improve sales conversion.

So – What Now?

It's time to learn!

As we've seen, many have relied on face to face meetings to help seal the deal. Shaking hands has served us well. But you need to develop something that can act as the best possible substitute; something that also develops trust. As we go through this guide, we will suggest some practical ways you can bring these substitutes onto the field of play, but there's a fundamental learning point to make first.

You must understand and make the most of your own communication style and you must recognise that your customers will also make sense of the world in their own way. Your way and their way may not be the same.

Some people prefer to look at things, others prefer to hear things. Another, albeit smaller group, will prefer something they can physically touch. This has big implications for how you demonstrate and sell your products and services to them.

It will make a huge difference to how much you get out of this book and how successful you are, if you can spend some time understanding your own preferred communication style and then how to recognise that of others.

Communication Styles

In the planning stages Mike and I discussed several examples of people we had come across with heavy preferences for particular communication styles. Mike had a case where someone with a heavy visual communication preference just wanted to see the brochure for Mike's new service. In my case, I recall explaining a new service over the phone, to a colleague who kept asking for a demo that they could play with – an example of a preference for tactile communication.

My own preference is always for something visual, whilst Mike prefers to listen and to talk. These differences between people mean that we need to have right type of marketing materials to pitch to them all equally effectively. This demonstrates how you may need to tailor your delivery to your audience.

We make sense of the world around us by using three key triggers for our stimulation: visual, auditory and tactile (a preference for touch, smell, and taste). All of us use all three, but we usually lead with one dominant preference. To help you, here is our rough guide.

Visually stimulated people prefer pictures, they like to show not tell. They love imagery. They will use gestures when they speak because the words themselves need to be augmented, like holding up three fingers in a presentation when there are three options. It is an unnecessary gesture – we can all count to three, right? But the spoken word is not enough. It's how they remember and how they make sense of things. In our new world, they will want to share screens with you. If you come across someone like this, you will show them you have built empathy when you say: "I see what you mean", and you provide them will visual imagery to demonstrate your offering.

Auditorily stimulated people love the spoken word. They love to talk. They love to listen to the radio, but they couldn't have music playing whilst working as they would lose concentration due to the need to listen. "I hear what you say". Discussing your offering may be more effective than using just images and diagrams.

People with a tactile preference like the experience of how things make them feel. They remember how they felt at certain events in their life. They rely on touch: they would prefer doing a puzzle to a crossword. They rely on non-verbal and non-visual communication to help them make sense of the world. You are going to have to work harder to gain their trust using phrases like: "I feel the same way". Are you able to give them something physical to demonstrate your product or service?

You may get clues to the customers preferences from any interaction that you have with them. Does their language, and their requests of you, give you any hints as to how they prefer to communicate? If so, follow that preference, whilst being prepared to deliver information to your customers in whichever form they prefer.

The benefit of understanding your customer's preferred communication styles is that you can tailor your message to them. If someone is visually driven, draw them a diagram or show them images rather than giving them long verbal explanations. Visual dominance will account for most of your customers, as it is the prevalent style – so if you don't know any better, default to that. However, conversely, if you are dealing with someone who has a different dominant communication style, you need to tailor your messages in a form that will be better received by them e.g. phone a person that shows a preference for auditory communication.

These changes to how we communicate with customers are likely to have the biggest effect on the minority of customers that prefer tactile forms of communication. These are the people that like to touch and feel things – this is perhaps an aspect that has been most severely impacted by the changes that have given rise to this book. Yet you can still try to tailor your messages to their preferred style. Can you produce sales and marketing materials which might appeal to them? Perhaps items sent by post might be a partial substitute?[iii]

Checkpoint Summary

1) Adapt your approach to your customer's preferred communication style.

2) Prepare your approach and your materials to support all communication preferences.

3) If their preference is unknown, default to visual representation as your primary focus.

You Can't Win 'Em All

As much as we would all love to close every sale, we have to face reality – there are some sales that you cannot win, no matter how hard you try – so stop feeling bad about those. If there is absolutely no desire, the customer will not purchase no matter how many incentives you give them. The following diagram illustrates that of all the sales opportunities you get, they are divided into three categories:

YOU CAN'T WIN 'EM ALL

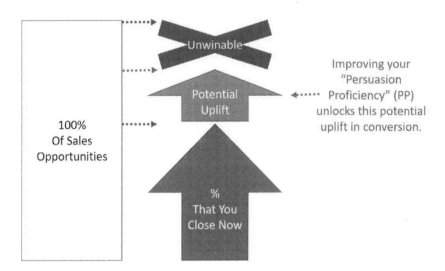

There are those you close now, those that you could close with an uplift in your PP, and those sales that are just "unwinnable". The unwinnable sales could be those where the customer has no intention of buying at present, something that simply cannot be overcome no matter how proficient you are. You need to recognise these and move on to spend your time on more profitable activities.[iv]

The Fallacy Of Sunk Effort

You may have heard of the "fallacy of sunk costs"? This is demonstrated by gamblers who continue to chase their losses, or people that overeat at a buffet because they have already paid the entry fee and feel they need to get their money's worth. The costs are already sunk (spent), continuing to spend more can be counterproductive. However, they feel the weight of what they have already invested, often so much so that they continue to do unproductive things because of that feeling.

A tweak on that well-known phrase is the "fallacy of sunk effort", continuing to chase after those unwinnable customers due to the amount of effort that you have already invested in them. It is a poor use of your time, but salespeople often feel compelled to do so. That effort has already been expended – it is gone. It is more efficient to write off the sunk cost of that sale and expend your future efforts on pursuing another - instead of continuing to expend effort on a sale that should really be classed as unwinnable.

That said, you may be able to creates some "low effort" approaches to keep in contact with customers that are currently unwinnable e.g. a regular email update to all your prospects. Such actions can be distributed liberally as it requires minimal additional effort to add another customer to your mailing list, and you never know when a customer's situation may change.

This perfectly illustrates how hard it is to let go of a potential customer you have been chasing for months. It feels like failure to admit there's no chance of gaining them as new business now, doesn't it? You must let them go, but as Glenn says, keep in touch in such a way that keeps you in their mind. Another approach that helps with priorities is to ask yourself "have I put my time where the money is?" It is the essence of effectiveness.

The "money" will most likely lie in the most rewarding sales, in your case that could be the biggest value sales or the longest potential contract period etc. So, the priority should become allocating most of your effort to winning those high value situations, rather than expending equal effort regardless of the potential reward.

Shortening The Sales Process

Time to take another look at your performance and be honest about the fundamental skill that you possess. Look at the previous diagram. Isn't this the most obvious illustration of possible improvement: If you can convert more opportunities (sales leads), you will be more successful. You would be rightly indignant if you thought the money you have spent on this book had been wasted if all we did was tell you to be better at conversion, and that was the secret.

And yet, somehow it is! But just telling you is not going to help you. The sales process has been shortened in a way previously thought impossible. Our system will help you maximise your chance of winning new business but be in no doubt the new normal presents you with a fantastic opportunity to take advantage of the truncated process. Aspire to use our system to increase the percentage that you close.

An important part of successful selling is focusing your efforts on productive tasks. Documenting why a few people didn't want your product produces nothing but a good paper trail. Of course, we need to have some ability to record and learn from outcomes, but a comprehensive report on why someone didn't buy is seldom productive. Refocus that time on developing new prospects and focus the most effort on those sales that offer the biggest rewards.

Time to Be Realistic

And honest. Some salespeople love to have long pipelines. Sales management can mean challenging the salesperson in a case-by-case review of their pipeline that includes suggestions or instructions. Our system is going to help you with those meetings, if you follow the system and learn to master it, you will uncover the unwinnable proposals much earlier than you might have done in a longer process that had involved numerous calls or visits.

Put simply, this is a wonderful opportunity to move your sales prospects to a decision point, more quickly than you did before. And if you have learned to use the principles in this book, to recognise and correctly move the weights on the balance, you will save time when you acknowledge that some opportunities can't be closed at the present time. Your closing techniques must be both empathic to the situation but also to drive more swiftly to a conclusion: ultimately, do you want it or don't you?

You will come across sections of sections of this book where you will learn how asking for the business is sometimes a really powerful approach for you to use, but know that this book does not set out to teach you the skills of pipeline management or deal progression.

Checkpoint Summary

1) Some sales are unwinnable, identify them and focus on more productive activity.

2) Apply your effort to the objective, building a sales pipeline, not documenting failures.

3) Expend the most effort on the sales that offer the greatest reward.

Relationship Building

What is relationship building?

Let's wind back to this part first before we go any further. It's important to recognise that whilst building a relationship with a prospect is a proven closing technique, you can't think of it as a one-way street. In fact, that could hinder you. You must see this from the very opposite end of the telescope. Its less about the prospect liking you and more about them feeling validated or appreciated by you and your interaction with them.

Let me explain. Unless you have a serious personality disorder like narcissism, humans want to be liked. If you know anyone who is heavily into approval-seeking behaviour, they need to be liked.

Because this is a business book and not a dating manual, we call it "affirmation". It's a professional goal you are setting here. Although if you can learn this and put it into practice, it may improve your personal relationships with friends and loved ones!

You aren't trying to build a personal relationship with your prospect, but you will improve your chances of a good outcome if they can feel affirmed by their interaction with you. The Ladder of Affirmation shows you that it's achievable in step by step increments.

So how do you do it when you cannot meet face to face?

The New Normal

Many of you reading this will have used the techniques we're about to explain. Some of you will do them naturally. Anyone who has highly developed interpersonal skills will say this is plain common sense. Yet check it out the next time someone is selling you something. Do you feel they listened to you, understood, validated, and respected you and were they sincere when they did so?

Failing to nurture these feelings in your customers, not showing them, they are understood, appreciated, and valued can have a negative impact on your ability to sell to them. They will go elsewhere because if you are not prepared to look after your customers, someone else will.

Lost Communication

I have bad news. The communication required for relationship building can be deconstructed into three parts, each of which has a weighting:

Less than a tenth of your message is comes from the words you use, over a third comes from the tone of your voice. And more than half comes from your non-verbal communication: your facial expressions and body language. In the new normal, maybe you can see the size of the task to overcome? More than half of what you have previously relied upon may now be lost if you are "on camera". Everything you learned about matching and mirroring is going to be blunted. It's not going to be completely useless in a video call, but it may be much less effective.

I can hear telesales professionals start to express their disagreement and probably pride at this point: "we never use over half (the non-verbal part), we never meet the customer and we are successful! Are you sure this is right?"

This gives a clue to the two key points.

You must craft your message so that it lands better.

You must hone your interpersonal skills to get better at listening and to further to climb the Ladder Of Affirmation. What can you learn from those telesales people? We will look at that later when we consider how to structure you message for maximum impact.

The question it raises for me is to what extent that additional segment of communication would either improve, or perhaps detract from, the success of those people that are skilled at telesales? Phone based selling is a different skill to selling F2F, but to some extent I suspect that the telemarketers will find that they are already a few steps ahead of the F2F salespeople, in the process of adapting to the new environment.

One of the major challenges in phone-based selling is that you are often unknown to the customer, and they may feel they owe you nothing. Not even the courtesy of a few seconds of their time, to hear your pitch. It's far easier to say "no" to someone that is not stood in front of you, and termination of the conversation is at the press of a button. The customer may even already have a predisposition against telemarketers generally, a medium that has been overused, which makes the task even more difficult. Despite this, some people are phenomenally successful at phone-based selling, so there is something to learn from them.

How do they engage in relationship building so rapidly? There are techniques e.g. "can you help me please?". That simple phrase imbues the customer with power, they feel like you think that they hold the answers.

It also has a challenge, "can you". We are all schooled to help others, and this simple phrase speaks to that part of us that wants to help other people and has been brought up to help others wherever we can. Once someone has agreed by answering in the affirmative, their psychology will be predisposed to carry out their stated obligation and continue to help you. OK, again there are no guarantees, but PP is all about improving your percentages by adjusting at the margins.

Emotional Drivers

Understand that your prospect's decision-making is motivated by emotional drivers as well as rational ones. In the case of a car sale, the rational driving force may be that the customer needs transport. However, the more powerful emotional driver may be that their friend has just bought a car, and they want the same model. That's why it's worth the effort in climbing the ladder. Its where the heaviest weights may be found.

Checkpoint Summary

1) "Relationship building" is a vital part of increasing your PP.

2) Large parts of communication are lost when we are limited to phone or video conferencing.

3) Craft your message to help make up for this, and improve your PP.

4) Remember that emotional drivers may carry more weight than rational drivers.

The Old Normal

"People buy people" is one of the go-to sales clichés you hear the most. Because it's true. I once managed a salesman whose performance was so good; he was like three people. He broke every record in the company and many in the industry, yet it was his first "proper" job in sales. Glenn once asked him for his secret: could he distil this into something that could be copied? "I just get them to like me" came the pithy reply.

Of course, the real answer is far more complex. To help us we need to unpick it and then to develop a solution that works with or without face to face meetings.

Clearly, you are unlikely to buy from someone you don't like, but you might if there are other pressures at play e.g. an item is in short supply. In general terms though people like to buy from people they like, and relationship building is all about getting people to like you, whilst also making them feel that you like them.

We need understand the psychological processes that make a person warm to another person and create that connection, even if it's not a deep friendship, but more of a short-term relationship. One aspect of that process is the use of affirmation to demonstrate to your customer that you respect them, appreciate them, and understand them. These are the foundations of creating even the most superficial relationship with another person.

I would mention here that when we talk about "superficial" relationships, we are not implying that there is any dishonesty. It may be a professional relationship with a colleague, rather than a deep, long-term personal friendship. Superficial just means that it's not the deepest of connections, it does not mean that it is not genuine. In fact, a key facet of selling is that if you are not genuine, people will probably see through any façade, and it will likely work against you.

So, to consider how to best use Affirmation to help your prospects to buy from you. This can be a powerful weight that tips the balance in favour of the sale.

The Ladder Of Affirmation

To help with visualisation of this, the next diagram is the **Ladder of Affirmation***:*

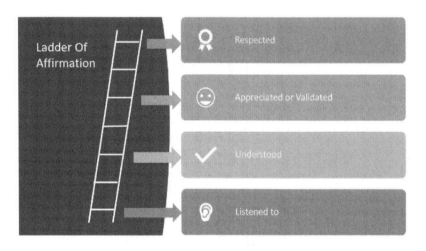

"Seek first to understand, then to be understood". You may have heard that before. But have you done it? In a sales environment it's tempting just to "pitch in" and start talking. Imagine how that comes across in a non F2F environment. You may have to take turns as the technology may not allow you both to speak at once. This gives you the perfect opportunity to listen and to show you are listening. You can then reflect what you have heard your prospect say, to further move up the ladder.

Many good salespeople open a meeting with something like "ok, tell me about your business". In the new environment, you should consider making a virtue of letting your prospect tell you by saying something like "Ok let me listen to you first". Then you can give them the summary later. If you have done this properly, as well as hearing them say "that's right!" you should find them asking for your opinion, inviting you to say how you might solve their problem. Because if they feel respected, they will want to offer you something in return.

Look at the previous diagram. It illustrates how using empathic listening can move you incrementally up the ladder. So now we will discuss each step, in turn.

Listened To

The first thing to note is that they do the talking. If your idea of a successful meeting is where you get the chance to pitch and then ram home your message to a close, you are reading the wrong book. If you listen correctly, they will tell you all about themselves or their business and what is needed. This will help you with closing the sale. We'll come back to closing later.

To show you are listening, you must reflect what they are saying to you. This is sometimes called "mirroring". To practice this skill outside of the business environment, get someone to tell you about something they are really interested in, or a story about something they really enjoyed like a holiday or a favourite gig.

Set the exercise up by asking them to tell you all about it: the build-up, the finer details, who went with them and especially how they felt.

As they speak, follow their interest, use their language to simply reflect your understanding. Give them their own words back. If they say, "it was the best gig I've ever been to" a good response would be "Wow, the best". Don't turn your responses into questions, In fact, don't ask questions at all. It's hard to do as simply repeating what they say can sound false and ungenuine. I absolutely guarantee you that the first time you do it, you will want to try and direct the narrative by saying things like "so what happened next?" DON'T! if they pause, simply encourage them by saying things like "Go on" or better, "tell me some more about that". If you start asking probing questions, you will ruin the listening dynamic as they will simply feel it is you who's in charge of the conversation. If you are asking them about things you are interested in, their narrative will falter, and you won't even have reached the first stage. Try it with someone you know well and treat this as practice for the sales situation where your task will be to follow their interest and use their language.

Understood

This is the natural consequence of your empathic listening. Because you have simply reflected their feelings, followed their interest, and let them talk without probing or directing, the other person will feel listened to AND understood. They will think it's a great conversation whilst, it isn't – it's their monologue with your encouragement.

This supports the salespersons need to hear the thoughts and views of the customer, rather than imposing their own assumptions about what is important, which can turn out to be incorrect.

Appreciated Or Validated

This is the subtle next step. To do this successfully you have to use a technique called "precis interrupting" that is, offering a summary of what the person has just said. You may do this all the time anyway. Let's carry on with the "favourite gig" example that you are going to use to practice this. They are telling you about the wonderful venue, the thrill of seeing the band take the stage, the excitement of their first song and how they always loved that track and they started singing along. You "top" their narrative by interrupting the flow with "it was dream start to the gig for you". Notice how all you said was a summary of what they had been saying to you and crucially, don't ask a question. At this point they should say something like "that's right!".

This is difficult to do sincerely. You will know if you got it right because your interruption will encourage their narrative even more.

Respected

If the person you are listening to feels validated by your approach and appreciated by your comments, they will feel respected. You have encouraged them. You have coaxed their feelings out without probing and dominating and most importantly, you have not projected your own life onto them. You should never say "oh yeah, I've done that" or "the best gig I went to was...". If they feel you respect them, they may ask you for your experience.

Even if they don't ask you, the objective has still been achieved. You will have learnt something about your customer and made them feel respected at the same time.

The Business Context

This all sounds very fluffy and supportive doesn't it? But how are you going to make this work in the world of business. As I said, the examples in the previous sections are only intended to serve as practice for you. But is it that easy to get your customer to start upon a business narrative that you can reflect, then interrupt and for them to feel respected? Yes of course!

Try asking them about where the business started and where they see the company going – what are their plans? A successful salesperson I managed used to do this every time by asking "What's your ideal exit?" No entrepreneur alive will be able to resist telling you where they want to go and whether they are planning a trade sale, an acquisition, a family handover, or to be bought out by their largest competitor. In answering your question, they will reveal things about themselves that will be priceless intel about what is important to them. Follow that interest, use their language, and interrupt them to give them a summary of their own ideas back, and you will have climbed to the top of the ladder.

I Know What You're Thinking

Another part of building a relationship is to recognise that people tend to like people that are similar to them. If you can demonstrate that you think along the same lines as somebody else, it can help build the relationship with that person as you are demonstrating that you are alike. That can be difficult to do with people that you have only just met, or don't know that well. However, there are ways of building that connection with people that you don't know very well.

One technique that many mentalists use is to listen to what a person says and play parts of that back to them. This makes it appear that they are saying things which line up with what that person already thinks. Another facet of human behaviour is that people like to maintain direction. Once a person feels they agree with what you are saying, they are less likely to pay attention to anything that contradicts that original notion.

A similar technique can be applied to sales. This is part of exhibiting empathy when listening to someone. By carefully listening to what the customer is saying and then taking the opportunity to reflect back parts of their own dialogue to them, you can create a situation where the customer feels, like Mike said, that you are speaking their language. This creates trust and is a key part of relationship building.

Furthermore, once a customer is convinced that you are the right partner for them, their psychology will press them to maintain that direction, rather than change their mind. Despite what you might think, the last thing that we like to do is change our minds. We are far more comfortable maintaining our opinions, to the extent that we will actively look for positives to advocate our original opinion, whilst playing down information that contradicts that original opinion.

Overcoming The Awkwardness Of Selling

One of my colleagues told me that they did not feel comfortable selling to customers. Their background was in customer service, so they felt that selling was at odds with the customer approach that they were accustomed to offer. In one simple adjustment I put them in a position where they became comfortable with the selling role. All I told them was to place themselves on the same side as the customer and help the customer make the best decision. Instantly they were transformed from the image they dreaded of a shiny suited salesperson into an expert that provided customer support, a role they felt much more comfortable with.

The key to the approach is to put yourself on the same side as the customer, so that you are not in a hostile confrontation with them. Instead, you are their ally, helping them to make the right decision and solve their problems and issues. You may find that a simple reframing of your role from being a salesperson to providing expertise, is enough to both change the way that you tackle a sales situation and overcome the potential negativity that a customer may perceive from having someone selling to them.

Projecting Confidence

There are no "dead cert" sales techniques, no magic formulae that you can follow towards making a sale every time. It is more a case that each technique may contribute a few percentage points towards an overall improved sales performance – it is all about playing the percentages so that you maximise your overall chances of success and in some circumstances, those few extra points might be enough.

People respect and are prepared to be guided by people they perceive as being experts. If you show a lack of confidence in your products and services, or your performance as a salesperson, it will have a negative effect on your customers.

Whilst you should not appear overly pushy, as that will cause a customer is close down, you need to demonstrate an element of confidence in yourself, and your offerings, in order to be perceived as credible by the customer. You will only be attributed expert status in the eyes of your customers if you project confidence.

Another important part of your approach to how you handle interactions with customers is to avoid appearing that you are desperate for the sale. If a customer believes that an item is in short supply, they are more likely to buy. If your behaviour as a salesperson demonstrates that you are desperate for a sale, their assumption is likely to be that you have not made any other sales, this will be working against you creating a barrier on the negative side of the sales balance.

Conversely, someone that demonstrates that others have already purchased, overcomes that barrier, and tips the balance towards making the sale. People believe in safety in numbers, if others have bought or given favourable reviews, they are more likely to purchase. To that end you might want to consider how to introduce customer reviews and testimonials into your sales process. This can be far more subtle than printing out reviews to send to them. It can be introduced in how you speak e.g. small talk about customers you have recently spoken to that have just purchased.

On the subject of confidence, don't reveal your weaknesses through a lack of confidence or embarrassment. When someone says "please excuse my awful outfit" attention is drawn to their outfit. It may well have been overlooked had attention not been drawn to it. The same applies to sales. Don't draw attention to the things you see as weaknesses through a lack of confidence. This doesn't mean don't head off possible objections in your pitch. The difference is that there can be a positive effect from getting out in front of a potential problem. That is not the same as just highlighting weaknesses as you are embarrassed.

Checkpoint Summary

1) Relationship building is more difficult if you can't get face to face, but it's still possible.

2) Use the Ladder of Affirmation to make customers feel: listened too; understood; appreciated and respected.

3) Place yourself on the same side as the customer, helping solve their problems and providing expertise.

Agenda Setting

Agenda Setting is about creating an environment where a customer is predisposed to purchase, prior to an actual interaction with the customer. It's the groundwork that you can do in advance to improve your chances of success.

How Do I Set The Agenda?

Before we explore that, let's ask a better question: **Why should I set the agenda?** *By setting the agenda ahead of any interaction, you are already contributing towards tipping the sales balance in favour of making the sale.*

Powerful psychological forces can be brought to bear to help you achieve higher success before you meet someone or interact with them. I have successfully employed this technique numerous times. The first move you make, the first idea you focus on, will change the way that people receive and feel about what comes next. So, find ways of framing the debate to focus on that which will predispose the customer towards buying. Giving a subject attention will make it important.

You may do this anyway without knowing it. I'll give you a personal example. I wanted to go away with my golfing buddies for a three-day holiday in France. I was worried about telling my wife how much it would cost. So, I came home with a bunch of flowers. My wife is much too smart to think I was giving her flowers just because I love her. She saw them and said, "What have you done and what do you want?" Then I launched into my golf holiday pitch and she eventually agreed it would be a great idea for me to go!

OK, so this example is extreme, because my wife knows me all too well, but you can see that what I was trying to do was to deliver my request as part of a construct that would predispose her to favourably consider what was coming next. People unkindly call it "softening up" and you have probably already thought of your own examples when you have experienced it or used it yourself.

Now think about how you can apply that to the business of sales. Specifically, can you focus your prospect's attention on some aspect of your product or service that you feel will carry the heaviest weight in their decision to buy from you. Understand that I'm not talking here about matching or meeting your prospect's aspirations. Setting the agenda for a meeting helps you direct the debate into the area that you want it to go. Also understand this is not a guarantee of success: it only boosts the possibility. Now let's go back to the first question of how to set the agenda.

Agenda Setting Technique

Before the meeting, you must deliver your bunch of flowers. One way to do this is what we call Agenda Setting Technique. Is there something you can get your prospect to think about before the meeting? Something that will prepare them to better appreciate what you are going to tell them about your company? Something that puts them in a state of mind to consider more favourably what you are going to say?

This example will hopefully explain what I mean, then you will have to think of something relevant to you.

I knew a lady who sold insurance against bad debts if customers failed to pay. Before every meeting she would send her prospect a short paper warning about a seeming "blue-chip" business that ran out of cash very quickly and failed before any credit reference agency could downgrade their ratings and advise caution. The articles also told of consequential losses where suppliers (who didn't have insurance of course!) could not survive the loss of such a customer and ceased to trade. The message was clear: you don't have a crystal ball and you should protect yourself and your business.

To improve her chance that this was read in advance and hence the prospect was already thinking they couldn't afford to be without insurance, she used a little flattery. "I think this is a really important article and I'd like to know your opinion on it. When we meet, can I please have your honest feedback about it?".

Not only was she setting the agenda, but our insurance salesperson was also making the prospect feel they had a chance to give their opinion, even if they thought the article was rubbish. They are going to be listened to, not sold to. It would also force the objections to the surface quickly when the meeting started. This sets a whole different agenda and applies some more subtle contributors to the positive side of the sales balance.

Note – some research for you. Look up Ben Feldman. Some people consider him the world's greatest life insurance salesman. You will come across examples of how he out-performed everyone else in the whole company in a competition he took part in when he was in hospital calling new prospects on the phone.

Most commentators agree the secret of his success could be distilled to an approach that he used to get his prospects to see insurance differently. Of course, he wanted to overcome any objection to cost, but he also wanted to make customers think that life insurance had human qualities. He likened it to a person on whom you can rely to take care of your family when you're dead and gone. A trusted friend whose very presence makes you feel better about the fate of your loved ones, because he or she will step up and look after them.

This is an excellent example of how to place yourself on the same side as the customer. You are not an adversary trying to sell them anything, you are introducing them to a friend that will help them – your product or service.

Now think about your own situation, what you want your prospects to think about before they first experience your message and what articles you could send them, maybe a YouTube video, that sets your agenda. As an example: If you don't want your price challenged in the meeting, then find something that focuses on the importance of quality or of safety in numbers. Research is required here.

But do yourself a favour and don't make the article a thinly disguised advert for your company. Don't send a testimonial from an existing customer and on no account send your brochure.

This doesn't set an agenda, at least not one that will be a contributor. The message your prospect will receive is that the sales pitch has already started. You haven't listened to them yet, or sought to understand their business, but you're the type of person who doesn't want to debate but just wants to dominate. That's like removing all your weights before you start, and you will find it almost impossible to replace them effectively and you may have reduced the probability of agreement.

If you don't have such sales collateral, then you should spend some time thinking about how to acquire it, author it or get an expert to write it.

So, remember, get your prospects to think about the important parts of your message in advance and find ways to convince them they should spend time considering it. You will notice a huge difference.

Obligation

If you are given something, you are more likely to return the favour and respond in kind. This effect can form part of agenda setting. As a result of giving something to your customer, they may feel in your debt and they will be more likely to purchase from you as a result. This does not have to be something of high value. A coupon or a business card can be very small-scale example of things that you can give a customer. The relevant article from the press we discussed above, or one that you come across that is relevant to something the customer said, could be a great examples of how you could invoke this principle at minimal cost.

If you feel that you are indebted to someone else, you are more likely to oblige them, and that could mean more likely to purchase.

This is one of the most widely used forces of influence in the world of selling. If I give you something for free, you will feel obligated towards me and will want to respond in kind. It's been tested time and again.

Think about corporate entertainment: You are my client. I take you to a high-profile rugby match. We have a good lunch beforehand, good seats and drinks afterwards. It's a memorable day. When I next call you to ask you if you want to upgrade or buy more from me, I am pressing home the advantage of the goodwill I have created. It's so powerful that there are laws against it: declarations must be made as to the value of hospitality so as not to be classed as "undue influence". But the fact is that even a small concession can create an obligation. In a negotiation, I gave up something for you, what have you got to give to me? It can be a contributor. Use it.

Sowing The Seeds

I would just like to add that agenda setting can be a very subtle adjustment. Whilst sending physical items, as Mike suggests, is a great way of influencing a customer, it can simply be in what you say. "Sowing seeds" is one way of achieving this. By dropping seeds (points) into an exchange or conversation, the customer can pick up on those points and they may continue to be influenced by them. For example, if you call someone about buying bad debt protection insurance, and you open the conversation with an apparently off-hand remark about your previous customer, who just took out a policy after suffering a large bad debt, it's a cautionary tale. It may be enough to start the customer thinking "if someone else has taken a bad debt, perhaps I will". It also references another customer purchasing, which in turn makes this customer feel more comfortable, as they will tend to prefer to follow in the footsteps of others. These techniques are subtle but can be highly effective.

Checkpoint Summary

1) Set the agenda in advance of any interaction, to sow seeds in the mind of your customer that make them more likely to purchase.

The Tipping Point Sales System

Let's recap.

We have covered what has changed for salespeople. To quickly summarise:

Selling without shaking hands has become the new normal – not in every situation, but in enough instances to make it imperative for you to learn how to adapt.

Handshakes are a highly evolved symbol of human behaviour and we have relied on them to signal mutual consent and agreement. You need to recognise the need to develop something to take their place.

If you relied heavily on relationship building as the most powerful tool in your sales toolbox, your need will be greater than others who haven't used it so much. There are different ways to affect the outcome, you may be able to add some new tools to your toolkit.

Non-verbal communication is the majority of how your message is received. Without meeting someone, you must focus more on how you say things and craft your message in advance, and develop your PP.

You will need to understand your own communication style and preference for processing information. Then you will need to recognise what your sales prospects prefer and will find most appealing.

The sales process is going to be shorter. Prospects may tend to decide quicker because the situation demands they adapt. Entrepreneurs want to seize opportunities and you need to offer them the chance to.

Equally the situation demands that you create empathy: you don't want to be seen as a vulture. So, you need to work on an interpersonally savvy way to affirm what your prospect wants but be realistic with the management of your sales process: You can't close every deal.

...SO, THE SOLUTION IS....

Improve your Persuasion Proficiency. Use what you are about to read to create a simple way to see the process, the interaction, and the opportunity to successfully sell using our system. Place yourself on the same side as your customer, helping them solve their problems. Ready?

How The Tipping Point Sales System Works

In an environment where "relationship building" is no longer sufficient to rely upon in order to make sales, we need a new model that can also function in a situation where we may not be able to have face-to-face contact, or even speak with our customers.

To arrive at such a model, we had to strip back the sales process, the persuasion process, to understand exactly what is going on. When elements of the traditional sales approach are stripped away, it is no longer enough to muddle through using your "like me and buy from me" skills. In situations where you can't necessarily compel someone with your personality, you need a deeper knowledge of the dynamics at play in every sales exchange, so that you can adapt your approach. This depth of understanding can be applied to all situations that involve persuading other people, not just sales, however that is the purpose that we are focusing upon.

Our tipping point sales system focuses on the dynamics that underpin any interactions where you are looking to persuade, or influence, another person. This makes it ideally suited to describing the forces at work when entering any sales negotiation. It also enables you to simply understand the "adjustments" you need to make to tip the balance in favour of making the sale.

When we talk about making a sale, It is not always the point at which you exchange goods or services for money with the customer. For instance, in my business, it would be the point at which we introduce a customer to a third-party funder, for others it may be getting a signature on an order or taking a deposit. You need to identify what that success point is for you.

The system we have developed transcends any one sales technique, creating a framework into which all sales techniques can fit. It focuses on the dynamics that underpin every interaction, where influence is being brought to bear by one individual upon another. The objective of the system is to allow you to map any scenario where persuasion is involved and identify ways to "tip the balance" of the situation towards making the sale.

As we showed previously, you cannot expect to close every sale – some will always be unwinnable. However, you can stretch your performance to improve the overall proportion that you are able to convert into successful sales.

Our system is simple, but also ingenious at the same time. It involves you seeing any sales situation as a balance, like the one in the following diagram:

BARRIERS – Demotivating Factors
- Things which prevent a sale
  - E.g. lack of money

CONTRIBUTORS – Motivating Factors
- Things which help you get a sale
  - E.g desire to own the item

Success when
Tipping Point is
reached = SALE

The balance being between factors which will positively motivate someone towards purchasing e.g. needing the product, which we call "contributors", and the factors which are demotivating them away from selling e.g. the price. These we refer to as "barriers". We refer to all the factors on both sides of the sales balance as "weights".

Your objective is to understand where all the weights are placed along the balance and move them to reach the tipping point.

When I first started work for a large high street bank, managing some of their corporate clients, I went on a visit to meet an entrepreneur that had taken a very innovative approach and successfully adapted their core product to several different markets. The owner told me that whenever he was presented with a problem that needed to be solved, he would, "lay out everything about the situation and the answer will become clear". That is good advice, and exactly what we are going to do by prepopulating the sales balance model in advance of any interaction with the customer.

You can visualise those weights arranged along either side of the sales balance. The motivating weights are arranged to the right of the centre point, the point on which the balance pivots – which is called the "pivot point". The barriers are arranged to the left of the pivot point. The objective is for the right-hand end of the balance to move downwards after the balance reaches tipping point. This is when the customer decides to purchase – and you make the sale.

In a situation where the contributors have more combined weight than the barriers, the customer will inevitably make the purchase. Conversely, when the barriers carry more weight than the contributors, you will never convince somebody to purchase, and that sales transaction may fall into the unwinnable category that we described previously.

An example of this might be selling a house to a person that cannot get a mortgage and has no deposit, no matter how many contributors you load onto the balance, the sale is never going to be made, as that person has no way of paying. However, if the deposit is the only issue, there may be other options to be explored that could solve their problems e.g. a deposit savings club.[v] Which presents a solution that overcomes that barrier so it is no longer an unwinnable sale.

So it is useful to see the situation in terms of a balance and the smallest of influencing forces can cause that balance to tip or prevent it from tipping.

This type of model is very easy for you to jot down on a piece of paper, either before or during an interaction with the customer – you might even use it if you are not going to interact with the customer at all. This could be if you are constructing say an advert that is going to be shown online. Using the system enables you to prepare your approach, think about how you are going to influence the customer in order to maximise your chances of reaching the tipping point, where the customer goes on to purchase. If you are interacting with a customer, you can use the system before and during the conversation to guide your approach as to how you react to information about the weights affecting the balance. If you won't have the benefit of customer interaction, you might have to rely upon your own intuition to identify the weights, or perhaps market research which we will touch upon later.

This analogy of a balance is also very useful as it enables you to think about how you can move items around the balance in order to affect the overall equilibrium. We call these "adjustments". The objective of adjusting being to tip the balance towards a successful sale whereby the right-hand side of the balance moves downward. As the analogy also confirms, it's not about the number of items that you place on the balance, it's about their combined weight.

As with a seesaw in real life, the further that an item is placed from the centre, the more force it applies to the side where it sits. This is called the "principle of levers". If two objects of equal weight are placed either side of the pivot point, and uniform distances from the centre, the balance is in perfect equilibrium. If you move one item further away from the pivot point, this increases the amount of force that it applies to the balance, such that the side that it sits on moves downwards.

Conversely, if two objects of equal weight sit either side of the pivot point, at equal distances from the centre, and one is moved closer to the pivot point – that object exerts less force and the opposite side of the balance moves downward. This suggests that if ways can be found of moving items around the balance, which we call making "adjustments", the equilibrium of the balance may be able to be affected.

When applying this system to any situation, the first task is to populate the balance with details of the various weights that are having an impact on the customer's thinking. Once it has been populated, the next task will be to consider how these weights can be moved in order to maximise our chances of reaching the tipping point, where the sale is made.

There are likely to be some weights which are blindingly obvious, for example that the price of making a purchase is highly likely to be a barrier in most situations.

However, there will also be weights which are less obvious, and require you to project yourself into the position of your customer. Furthermore, there may be further weights that are invisible to you and are difficult, if not impossible to identify or anticipate – unless the customer alerts you to their existence.

Note: Go back to the Ladder Of Affirmation. If you have got the customer to talk about their business in such a way that makes them feel validated by you, they may be more prepared to tell you about these invisible weights.

So in order to start to populate the sales balance, the first task is to take a walk in the shoes of your customer and start to populate the weights that you would expect to be on either side of the pivot point, before you confirm those assumptions with the customer.

Identify The Forces That Are At Work

A first step is to sketch out the current position of the sales balance, identify the weights that are at work and estimate where the balance is – are you already near the tipping point with the right hand end sitting close to the ground? Or is the balance stacked against a sale, with the right-hand end sitting high in the sky?

Sketch out the elements and estimate where you are starting from, as demonstrated in the following diagram:

IDENTIFY THE "WEIGHTS" ON THE SALES BALANCE

BARRIERS – Demotivating Factors
- Things which prevent a sale
  - E.g. lack of money

CONTRIBUTORS – Motivating Factors
- Things which help you get a sale
  - E.g desire to own the item

Success when
Tipping Point is
reached = SALE

To have any chance of fully understanding the dynamics at play, you will also need to have a detailed understanding of your competitor's product or service offerings. Unless you know the competition you may be up against, you cannot appreciate how your offering will compare, and hence be perceived by the customer.

Know Your Competition

Understand your offering, and that of your competitors in detail. Otherwise, you cannot sell effectively. It's more than just knowing their name; it's about having a detailed understanding of how their products and services work.

I have worked with a financial services salesperson who is expert at this, he knows every nuance of his competitor's products and services, as well as his own.

His approach to sales is to utilise this knowledge to be able to outsell his competitors. He can tell the customer exactly how the funding levels are going to compare between different facilities, he knows how they might be affected by different nuances within the funding process. He can explain where his product will have advantages to offer the customer. This type of knowledge can be invaluable; indeed, it is hard to sell anything without at least a rudimentary understanding of your competitor's offerings, and how they compare to yours.

There is competition in every sector and unfortunately you are never able to sell in isolation. In fact, as the Internet has given customers instant access to information about you and your competitors, together with an expectation that they can utilise comparison and review sites, in order to assess and compare offerings.

So, you need to understand how your competitor's product offerings affect the sales balance. It is widely accepted that there are negative connotations associated with running down your competitors. However, a more subtle approach is to understand the intricacies of the products and services that they offer, so that you can use that knowledge to highly the benefits of your offerings, to your advantage.

There are some practitioners who say, "Don't ever ask for a comparison between your product and that of your competitors". Understand your advantages but simply don't even talk about what your competitors can or can't do. You may unconsciously be giving them greater weight.

In our sector, if a competitor's financing service does not allow you to upload your sales invoices, but your system does, that can create a significant time saving for your customers. It's just a case of promoting the benefits of your offering, rather than running down the offering of your competitor – which just sounds like sour grapes.

It is also important to be mindful that you do not become overly convinced of the weight of the benefits of your offerings. Whilst it is great to have a passion for the products and services that you are delivering, do not assume that they will weigh heavier on the sales balance than those of your competitors. In our sector, we often hear funders advocating the power of their brand in drawing in customers. Brands may be important in some situations, car brands and watch brands may carry a lot of weight. However, when you are talking about more transactional, commoditised products, brand may not carry the weight that you expect. Also, customers may not perceive the benefits of your brand or your products in the same way as you do. You may not have the level of brand recognition that you believe.

However, don't confuse this for not having total faith in your company and its products or that will be communicated to your customer in an instant.

In the sector that you operate, there may be technical nuances that are obvious to the expert but remain obscure to the uninitiated. Would you have known that a "120-day recourse period" was an advantage in my sector? Probably not, unless you were familiar with the invoice finance sector, in which case you would know that it could be a significant benefit. To the layman it has no value until it is explained. I suggest that you do not automatically assume that your weights when applied for the sales balance are going to be heavier than those of your competitors. The example is also a cautionary tale about the use of jargon. Technical terms and acronyms may have meaning to you, but your customers may need you to use layman's terms to explain what you are offering them.

Contributors

The "contributors" are all the motivating factors, connected to a sale, that are influencing the customer towards making the purchase. They appear on the right-hand (positive) side of the sales balance, as shown in the following diagram:

CONTRIBUTORS

IDENTIFY THE "WEIGHTS" ON THE SALES BALANCE

CONTRIBUTORS – Motivating Factors
- Things which help you get a sale
- E.g desire to own the item

An example of a contributor could simply be that the customer wants the product, it could be the fact that their friend already bought one, or that your product is currently on a "limited time only" offer. These weights sit on the right hand side of the sales balance, such that they are pressing down on that side of the balance and pushing the right-hand end of the balance downwards towards the point at which the sale is made.

There are a whole host of items that you may identify as being placed on that side of the balance. For example, they could include the customer's desire to possess the item. If you are talking about a car for instance the motivating weights could be as follows.

The most compelling need maybe their requirement for transport. It may be that they need a car to get to and from work. This would place the need for transport further away from the pivot point on the positive, right-hand side of the sales balance. This means that the item exerts a greater force towards reaching the tipping point, as the distance from the pivot point multiplies the effect of that factor. As you move an object away from the pivot point, towards the end of the balance so it exerts more downward force – it has more leverage. By making this type of adjustment, and moving the weight, the force exerted by a factor may be increased.

Taking the car example, there may be other contributors which are involved. These could include the desire to have a car that will look impressive to other people. In many sectors, the car that somebody drives is the first signal that colleagues will use to judge the success of that person. Hence, it being an impressive make, or specification could be an important issue. In a sales environment, it is often the case that a company's car policy will have a lot to do with attracting, and retaining, good salespeople.

Another motivating factor could be that the lease is up on their existing car. Now this could start off as one of those "invisible weights" that you are not aware of immediately. The only way of getting to understand the customer's situation is to communicate with them, to identify what the motivations are behind their interest. Asking open questions, that allow the customer to talk about their needs and requirements is the best way of understanding what these contributors may be. In the case of the car, you might ask "what is it that you're looking for?" An open question gives them scope to answer in any direction. A closed question e.g. "which model are you interested in?" is unlikely to reveal much information about their underlying motivations, as it only focuses only on one aspect, the model.

These types of invisible weights, may be the most highly motivating. This can place them on the far right-hand side of the sales balance. However, you also need to bear in mind that in many cases a customer may not want to reveal information which they feel could put them at a disadvantage. For example, by telling you that their lease is due to expire, they may be concerned that you will perceive them as desperate, take advantage of that situation, and they may not get the best price. Often this type of thinking can stop someone from declaring their real motivations. They key is to place yourself on the side of customer. Then, you are not selling - **you are helping them buy**. I have put that in bold to emphasise its importance. It is one of the most important concepts within our system.

If you have the benefit of a conversation with a potential customer, you can discuss their requirements with them, to identify the contributors. You can then place them along the right hand side of the sales balance, according to how much influence you feel they have on the purchasing decision – ideally you can get the customer to tell you how important each factor is. For example, the expiry of the lease may be the primary driving factor that is exerting the greatest force, moving the customer towards the tipping point. However, it may be the case that wanting a car that is going to look good is a far more influential emotional driver, as the customer is highly motivated by the respect they enjoy from their peers. Perhaps they don't even really recognise this themselves. In such cases, features such as the type of car, and specification may be more important than the timescale within which the car is going to be available. If the expiry of the lease is the most pressing factor, it may be that a customer is prepared to compromise on other aspects, to get a car as soon as possible. This is the type of situation where the buyer accepts a non-standard vehicle colour in order to be able to take immediate delivery without waiting.

Barriers

It is on the left-hand, negative side of the sales balance, that you place the de-motivating factors which we call the "barriers".

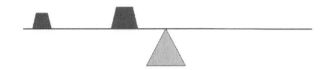

IDENTIFY THE "WEIGHTS" ON THE SALES BALANCE

BARRIERS – Demotivating Factors
* Things which prevent a sale
  * E.g. lack of money

These include all the factors which are dissuading the customer from purchasing. These could be aspects such as the price, wait times for delivery, types of product that they don't want, and even the hassle involved with making a new purchase. Or it could be alternatives that your competitors are offering.

Once again, you can place these items on the left hand side of the balance, with their distance from the pivot point adjusted to reflect the amount of influence that the factor has on the sale. Again, in an ideal world your communication with the customer will elicit the relative importance of the various weights, from their perspective. You may have to use your own intuition to judge the relative significance, and hence the relative positioning of these weights.

Price And Trust

In almost all sales situations, you can immediately assume that the issues of trust, and price will appear somewhere on the left-hand side of the balance. It is exceedingly rare for anyone to fully trust anyone that they just contacted, or to be prepared to part with any money that they do not have to. Therefore, this means you need to account for how you will address those two items, as a matter of course. Remember, you may know that you and your organisation are completely trustworthy, but unless you represent a well-known brand, you may be an unknown quantity to your prospective customers and trust will need to be earned. Even if you are representing a huge, well respected brand, trust on a personal level may still need to be earned.

Going back to the example of the sales person that focused solely on getting customers to like him, he went on to say: "get them to like you and they will buy from you, get them to trust you and they will buy more". It's a vital consideration – building trust, but how is it done? Acting with integrity, being genuine and placing yourself on the same side as the customer is a good start.

Adjusting The Barriers

In populating the barriers, let us look at an example. If when buying a car, the customer hates the colour red but that is the only colour in stock for the model that they want, the colour could be a significant demotivating factor. Therefore, it may be placed on the far-left hand side of the balance, such that it is the biggest barrier.

Other weights may be placed closer to the pivot point because they are less influential on the sale. For instance, if the customer does not have much of a budget to purchase, that may be a barrier. However, because they have some budget available, you may place that weight somewhere towards the pivot point, rather than being on the far extreme of the left-hand side of the balance. This means that it exerts less force against the sale than the items which are at the extreme end of the scale. It therefore follows that to try and move the balance in favour of a sale, the items that are furthest to the left of the scale are those on which you should focus first.

Removal of these items, which are achieving the greatest leverage against the sale, should be your top priority in trying to reach the tipping point. If it is not possible to remove these items, as you will see later, it may be possible to mitigate the impact that they have, and reduce their the amount of force that they are able to bring to bear on the negative side of the sales balance. This can be achieved by moving them towards the pivot point.

Whilst my simple example has involved the sale of a car, the same sales balance technique can be applied to any, and all sales interactions. Even in a situation where you are unable to speak to a customer, you can still make some inroads by defining the dynamics at work, by projecting yourself into the position of your customer. By placing yourself in their shoes, you can anticipate the factors that will be important to them and note down the various weights that you think would be at play within a situation. It is always best to get the customer's input for this definition stage; however, some benefit is derived from preparation by considering the weights at play yourself. This is of course something that you can do in advance of contacting a customer as it allows you to explore the weights in advance of any interaction. However, it will never be as effective as analysing the weights during the course of an interaction with the customer, even if it has to be via a discussion in a written format e.g. an online chat, an email exchange or a phone call.

Application To Promotional Materials

The system also has something to add in situations where you are not going to have any direct contact with customers, for example, if you are preparing an advert or even a post for social media.

If you were in the process of designing an online advertisement for say a business finance product, you might start by sketching out the sales balance, and trying to empathise with the customer, in order to understand the key weights that sit on either side of the sales balance.

In this example case, to the right of the pivot point you might place the contributor weights, including their need to improve cash flow. This could be a primary driving concern, which would place this item at the far-right hand side of the balance. This means that this item will have the greatest influence on reaching the tipping point, and achieving the sale.

Further towards the central pivot point may be other weights that are contributors, but have less impact on reaching the sale as they bring less force to bear on the situation. These could include weights such as getting a discount on the price. This may be motivating a customer to apply for finance, because they feel that the offer is perhaps time bound. However, the force exerted by the opportunity to receive a discount, may not be as much as that exerted by the overall driving need to improve company cash flow. In such situations, it could be that the customer could go elsewhere in order to gain more funding, hence better solve the cash flow problem, despite not being offered a discount on the fees.

In this way, you can see that the different weights may interact with each other. They each exert a different level of force on the positive and negative sides of the balance.

However, as we will see later, there are ways of changing the dynamics in these types of interactions. For example, adjusting so that weights that were previously seen as exerting a small amount of force in a given situation, can be exponentially magnified to multiply their effect. Similarly, barriers that were bringing a significant amount of force to bear on the balance, may be able to be moved closer to the pivot point, or removed totally, to move the balance further towards the tipping point.

Checkpoint Summary

1) Use the tipping point sales system to better understand the dynamics of selling.

2) Start by identifying all the "weights" that are in play, on the sales balance – both the contributors (motivating a sales) and the barriers (preventing the sale).

3) Assume trust and price WILL BE barriers and so seek to address them.

Confirming Your Assumptions

It can be a useful exercise to populate the sales balance prior to any interaction with the customer. This allows you to pre-think the weights that are likely to be at play, and decide on your strategy for tackling each of them.

However, there is no substitute for the benefits that will be achieved by discussing the weights directly with the customer. Whilst we can try to project ourselves into the position of somebody else, this is likely to lead to inaccurate interpretation of exactly what their opinions might be. Therefore, wherever possible, you should try to discuss the factors that are important with the customer, through whatever communication channels you have available.

The other important property of any balance is that a tiny amount of weight on either side, can have a dramatic impact on the overall outcome, as we will see later. Again, whilst you can try to anticipate the significance of any factor on the balance, the best way of gauging their relative weight, is by discussing them with the customer. You might ask for example, "which is more important to you? A or B?" This type of question might throw some light on the relative importance of different aspects and how much significance the customer places on each of them.

If you are struggling to get an answer from a customer to what appears to be a simple question, try stepping back and asking a question one step removed. For example, if they can't tell you whether A or B is better, maybe ask them "what's making you struggle with the decision?". You might learn something using this type of technique, something way more useful than just the answer to the question. It might reveal more about how they are thinking about the purchase. There may be another issue that you haven't even considered. Bear in mind that we have one mouth and two ears for a reason, so that we use them in those proportions – listen more, talk less and you will understand more about your customer's motivations.

Whilst the concept of having this type of discussion with the customer is perfectly possible in the "old world" of face-to-face discussions, and it may still be possible in the "new world of" video conferencing etc., there are other aspects of marketing and sales where you do not have the luxury of a discussion with the customer.

Much selling is now undertaken over the Internet, and your online material and content may be required to do the selling for you. When you are writing your pitch, perhaps in the form of an online post or advert, you only have your assumptions of the customer's influencing factors to go on, or do you?

Customer Research

It would be great to be able to speak to each individual customer, in order to understand exactly what the weights are that are affecting the sales balance, in their particular case.

This is not always possible, but an element of market research may be possible, in order to gauge the types of issues that are relevant to particular types of customers. OK, it won't be a perfect fit for every customer, but it is perhaps better than just using your own intuition.

If you were to place the different approaches along a continuum, at one end you may have using your own assumptions about what is, and is not, important to the customer. At the other end of the spectrum you may have speaking directly to the customer. Somewhere in the middle, is market research. This is a type of research is where you ask questions of customers similar to those that you are seeking to attract, so that you can understand more about the views that they have, their needs and their opinions.

This can put you in a far better position than just projecting your own assumptions onto your customers. It is highly unlikely that you will be representative of the segment of customers that you are seeking to attract, therefore, your thoughts about what is and is not important to them could be inaccurate. By questioning customers that are similar to those that you are trying to attract, you can form a far more representative opinion of the types of issues that are important to them.

Obviously, undertaking an in-depth piece of market research could come at a significant cost. That is great if you have the budget. If not, there are compromised approaches that you might consider. Perhaps you might choose to conduct a "rough and ready" version of a market research study yourself. This might involve calling a few companies, within similar segments to your customer, and getting a feel for their understanding of the issues there are relevant to customers like them.

If you have a draft version of an advert or other types of published material, it might be helpful to seek the opinions of your target audience. Again, even if full scale market research studies are out of the question, perhaps you could seek some initial feedback from the people you know, or a sample of people that fall within your target segment. This type of testing helps avoid mistakes and glaring errors that are obvious to people within that segment, but perhaps are not so to you.

When we talk about "segments" we are referring to groups of people or organisations that are similar. For example, it may be that you are targeting construction companies. These construction companies may all be small owner managed businesses. Therefore, it would be reasonable to contact a sample of owner manager construction companies, in order to get a general understanding of the types of issues that are likely to be important to them and how they would view your offering. It would be reasonable to expect that their views may be representative of the views of others like them.

If you are going to conduct any research, the considerations would fill another whole book in themselves. However, to give some quick guidance, consider three important issues.

Respondents

Firstly, make sure that the parties that you are contacting represent your target audience. If your product is for businesses, you need to contact businesses and not just members of the public. The more representative that your sample of respondents is, the more like your target customers they are, the more useful your research will be.

Medium

Secondly, consider the medium that you are going to use. Will it be a phone interview, or will you send a questionnaire in the post, or do you plan to use an online response form? Postal or online forms sound like a great idea, but will you get the level of engagement that you need? Most people are pressed for time and so you cannot assume compliance with your request, you may need to offer an incentive to receive a reply.

Questions

Thirdly, take care with the phrasing of your questions. Think carefully about the types of answers that respondents are likely to give to your questions. In some cases, you might want to limit them to yes or no answers, or to seek responses according to a predefined scale (e.g. on a scale of 1 to 10, with 10 being very important, how important is . . .). However, your best feedback may be gleaned by using open questions that give them the opportunity to say anything, which could include issues that you have not thought of.

Ignore the market research findings at your peril! I have watched several episodes of "The Apprentice" where candidates undertake market research, and then decide to overlook the results, giving priority to their own opinions about what is and isn't going to be important to customers. Normally with disastrous results.

Market research can alert you to significant issues with products that you are in looking to promote. I saw a great example of this many years ago, a company that were looking to promote the supply of lunchtime foods into the workplace. Curry was one of the options they were thinking would be a great choice for lunch, and so we conducted some research to understand customer's opinions. Curry is obviously an extremely popular option when eating out, and so one might assume that it would be a great lunch option. However, the market research showed very clearly that customers did not want to eat curry at lunchtime. The reason being the lingering aroma when they returned to the workplace. Nobody wanted to stink of curry all afternoon!

It is good practice to avoid questions where you ask people to compare your product to others. Make sure they only think about your product and its merits and do not invite comparisons to others. Retain their focus on what you are delivering.

Invisible Weights

"Invisible weights", are the factors affecting any interaction with the customer, that you are not aware of. These can have a dramatic impact on the exchange, and can weigh heavily on either side of the sales balance.

If you have done everything you can to reach the tipping point, but the balance just refuses to budge, seeming to defy the laws of gravity, there may be unseen forces at work against you. These may be invisible weights.

These weights may be identified in conversations with customers or as part of your market research. Often they may not be surfaced but can continue to weigh heavily on the balance.

A typical way that you may identify these invisible weights is when you have overcome all of the objections that appeared to be in the way of a sale, and yet the customer still doesn't want to commit. This could be due to something completely unconnected, and unknown to you which is holding the customer back.

Take the example of a car sale, the customer may be sold on that particular model and specification that you're offering, you have overcome their issues of price by arranging finance for them, and breaking down the cost into manageable chunks. However, they still are reluctant to go ahead with the sale. This could be due to invisible weights which are exerting influence.

In this example, maybe the customer needs to discuss the purchase with their partner. Maybe they don't want to mention this to you, as they see it as a mark of weakness. This is the typical type of invisible factor that could be at play but is not immediately obvious to you. Of course, you can probe, if you have the opportunity, to try and determine what those weights may be, but often they remain invisible. Just being aware that they might exist gives you the opportunity to understand why things may not be moving as you might have expected them to. In such scenarios, as you are aware that there may be invisible weights at play, you might choose to dig further, to try and surface them.

Inert Factors

Inert factors are all the information that you know by the customer, but which really appear to have no bearing on the sales balance. For example, you might know that the customer plays golf. When you first populate the sales balance, you may think that this factor is completely irrelevant. It neither motivates, nor demotivates the customer towards purchasing.

As part of the initial scoping out of the current sales balance status, you might note some of these inert factors in the centre, above the pivot point. It's just identifies that they are datapoints, or facts that you are aware of, but you don't believe they have any impact on the sale.

In the diagram below, you can see an example of the sales balance that has been mapped out. It has been populated with some contributors and barriers. You will see that the inert factor, in this example that "the prospect plays golf", has been placed in the centre at the top.

INERT FACTORS

Those that apparently have no bearing on the sale.

E.g. The prospect plays golf

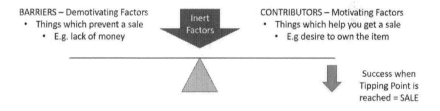

BARRIERS – Demotivating Factors
- Things which prevent a sale
  - E.g. lack of money

CONTRIBUTORS – Motivating Factors
- Things which help you get a sale
  - E.g desire to own the item

Success when Tipping Point is reached = SALE

We have termed these factors "inert" as and in the study of chemistry, inert substances are those which do not have any bearing on a reaction, they are chemically inactive. Therefore, anything which is known, but does not have any bearing on the sales balance can be considered an "inert factor".

Checkpoint Summary

1) Where possible confirm your assumptions about what's most important, ideally with the customer themselves.

2) If you are struggling to reach the tipping point, look for invisible weights that may be unseen and preventing the sale.

Adjusting To Change The Balance

Once you have identified the weights at work on the sales balance, you can start to think about making "adjustments". These are the actions that you take to change the relative impact of the weights, and to move the balance in the direction of making the sale. This could be by moving their position on the balance, removing them completely or adding weights to the mix. The first thing to recognise is that the weight of all the factors is not the same.

The Weight Of All Factors Is Not Equal

When you start to think about moving the weights around the balance in order to move it towards the tipping point, you should remember that not all weights are equal, and not all "adjustments" will have the same level of impact. The factors at work on the sales balance will have different relative weight, and so will have a greater or lesser effect on the balance. You might discount the price by a huge margin, but that will make no difference to someone that does not trust you. Indeed, a dramatic price concession could lead them to trust you even less and become more cautious about purchasing. Many people think that if it is too good to be true, it probably is.

The One Gram Weight

My father had a set of weighing scales that were used by jewellers to weigh gold. With the price of gold being so high, the tinniest quantity is valuable, hence the scales had some small weights. One of those was a single gram weight. It was tiny and looked like the smallest piece of tin foil.

If the dynamics are such that the customer is already at the point of equilibrium, the most minor of changes can be all that is required to tip the sales balance. In these circumstances, a small additional weight may be all that's required to tip the balance either way.

The concept of adding something to the positive side of the balance, that has little or no value to you, may be an attractive way of tipping the balance. Conversely though, failing to deal with a tiny grievance on the negative side, preventing the sale, can be very frustrating. I cannot tell you what the low value, yet critical one-gram weights are going to be. Just be aware to look out for them, as they can make the difference between success and failure.

The Heaviest Weight

So how can you cut through the process and head straight to the end game? Perhaps by identifying the most significant weights that are at work.

It is worth mentioning that there may be one, or a small number of weights, having an overly significant effect on the sales balance, such that they outweigh all the other weights. If you can identify the heaviest weight(s) you may be able to accelerate closing the sale by focusing on that item.

This is shown in the following diagram:

THE HEAVIEST WEIGHT

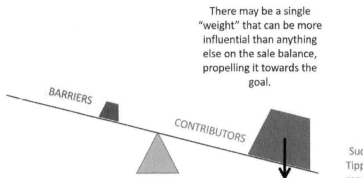

There may be a single "weight" that can be more influential than anything else on the sale balance, propelling it towards the goal.

Success when Tipping Point is reached = SALE

This may be a positive contributor, as shown in the diagram e.g. a benefit to your customer, or it could be on the negative side, a significant barrier that is stopping the customer from moving forward. By identifying these heavy weights early on, you can skip to the end game, without needing to address all other the other weights and the task of trying to influence their effects. Indeed, if you understand the most significant items affecting the customer's motivation, you may be able to stop worrying about other issues. For example, a plumber that is told that no one else can work on an urgent leak for several weeks, is not going to need to consider discounting the price for the job – they could even charge a premium and still close the sale.

In some instances, it may be that the heaviest weight is also an invisible factor, as described previously, or it may be blindingly obvious e.g. in the plumbing example, when the customer tells you that they are desperate. It could be that the heaviest factor is something that the customer does not want you to know about.

In the plumbing example, perhaps they don't want to mention the lack of competition, as they fear it will drive up your price. Keep a look out for these heavy weight factors as they could save you a lot of time, and even money. The best way of surfacing a hidden heavy weight factor is by engaging the customer in discussion where you probe to identify the various weights, as described previously – together with their relative importance.

Also remember that it's okay to come right out and ask the prospect "What's the most important aspect of this product/service/proposal for you?" it's like saying "if I can fix this, do we have a deal?" It might be cost, speed of response, flexibility, or quality. Of course, the others are important but in identifying the heaviest weight and then conceding it, don't let the prospect put all those other weights on the scale: some belong to you and are non-negotiable. Be bold!

Identifying Heavy Weights

If these heavy weights are not immediately apparent, there are ways that might help you identify the weights and adjustments that are likely to have the greatest impact, because there are a few factors that can have a disproportionately significant effect upon a customer. They are the factors that are most likely to make the biggest impact when you are trying to get the sales balance to tip in favour of a purchase. So, it would be wise to consider those factors and use them as a sanity check tick list every time you are thinking about what forces are at play, and what adjustments you are seeking to make to the balance.

There are some common threads that run through the weights that tend to weigh the heaviest on the sale balance. These are not "magic bullets" that will work every time, instead it is more the case that they are likely to be more effective than other factors. These highly effective weights include the following.

Short Supply

If something is in short supply, people feel more compelled to purchase it. You only need look at the 2020 "toilet roll fiasco", following the virus outbreak, to see that in action. For several weeks, the supermarket shelves were stripped bare of toilet rolls, an item that had always been in plentiful supply, as people started stockpiling them. This behaviour was driven by the fear that supply would dry up in the wake of anticipated lockdown, and disruption to supply lines. It was exacerbated by reports on the news and in social media about how supply was running out. During that period, I had several conversations with people that said something along the following lines.

"Isn't it ridiculous how people are panic buying all the toilet rolls. We had better order a few more this week just in case".

This statement encapsulates the principle of short supply. If people fear that something is, or will become scarce, they are more likely to purchase. This was the key factor in the plumbing example that I gave previously.

You might utilise this effect by offering, for example, a time limited offer. In the business finance sector, financiers often put an expiry date on offer letters to customers, as this invokes the perception of short supply. The customer fears the offer will expire if not accepted, and it might be taken off the table. This makes them more likely to purchase.

Relationship Building

This has been covered extensively above, but to recap in the context of what has the greatest effect in compelling people to purchase – people are more likely to buy from people they have established a relationship with. It's not a case of needing to be best buddies, but even in a professional context people prefer to deal with people that they know and have built a relationship with.

Endorsement & Safety In Numbers

This is a survival skill that is ingrained in everyone. If you see several others doing something, you are more likely to do the same. There is safety in numbers. People will seek out customer reviews for a product, and if they see several people speaking well of a product, they are more likely to purchase.

Similarly, people like endorsements. They prefer to deal with parties that appear to have the endorsement of people, or bodies, that they trust. Employing this factor could be as simple as showing that you are part of a recognised body, that you have won awards, or that you work in conjunction with say a government body. If your service or organisation is recommended by "experts", people are more likely to want to buy from you.

So, prioritise these factors when looking for the heaviest weights, as they are likely to be important in creating momentum within the sales balance.

Conversion Of Barriers

Returning to how we adjust the weights on the balance, let's start with the barriers. The objective is to remove the barriers, but there may be an even smarter approach that can be effective in some cases.

This is the art of "sales alchemy". Turning barriers into contributors – showing the customer how something that they thought was a barrier to the sale, was a contributor all along.

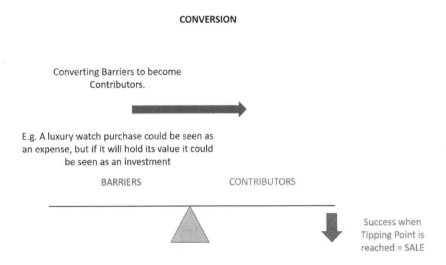

CONVERSION

Converting Barriers to become Contributors.

E.g. A luxury watch purchase could be seen as an expense, but if it will hold its value it could be seen as an investment

BARRIERS   CONTRIBUTORS

Success when Tipping Point is reached = SALE

Of course, this needs to be done with a certain amount of integrity to carry any weight, have any leverage and positively tip the sales balance. You may have heard the comical estate agent ploy of describing a derelict building as "ideal for the DIY enthusiast". People will almost always see through phoney sales blarney, but there are ways of achieving this type of sales alchemy, the conversion of barriers into contributors, without jeopardising the sale by using slick sales patter.

In the business finance sector, we can sometimes move the issue of price all the way from the negative, left-hand side of the sales balance to the positive right-hand side. It can be converted from a barrier, into a contributor towards the customer purchasing. This is done by identifying the benefits as outweighing the cost. This puts the product into a cash positive situation, transforming the issue of price from a barrier, to a contributor. This is the ultimate example of successful conversion.

One of the financial services that our brokerage company offers, is a financial product for businesses called factoring. It offers customers finance against unpaid invoices to customers, and a credit control service to collect in those unpaid invoices. Of course, this comes at a cost, a fee that the customer pays to use the service. Therefore, when you first start speaking to a customer about factoring, the price typically sits on the left hand side of the sales balance, a barrier to purchasing.

However, one of the aspects of this particular product is that the credit control service means that this task is undertaken by the finance company. This means that the customer does not need to undertake the work themselves, and hence does not need to employ credit controllers to carry out this function. This can be a significant financial benefit. Let's say that the cost of a credit controller is say circa £25K per annum. If the factoring fees are less than £25K (they are likely to be significantly less), it creates a cash positive benefit to the customer such that the value of the benefit outweighs the cost of using the service. In this way, a factor that could initially be considered a detractor, can be converted to a contributor as by taking the service, the customer will save money.

Removals

Removal is the next option to deal with a barrier when conversion is not possible. Removal is where an item is completely removed from the negative side of the balance. You may not be able to convert them all the way into a contributor (as described above), but you can at least remove them from the equation.

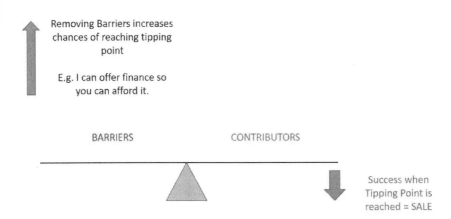

REMOVALS

Removing Barriers increases chances of reaching tipping point

E.g. I can offer finance so you can afford it.

BARRIERS   CONTRIBUTORS

Success when Tipping Point is reached = SALE

An example might be if the customer does not have the cash to purchase immediately, but they need the goods up front. This is a common problem for businesses that need to buy raw materials, to manufacture products, before they can sell them on and get paid. That would be a significant barrier to them proceeding. If you were able to offer them a credit account, such that they had a period of time to pay, this might enable them to receive customer payments in respect of their own sales in order to settle your account. This could effectively remove the issue of not having the cash completely from the sales balance.

Remember not to make concessions without seeking to close the sale on a conditional basis, "if I give you X, have we got a deal?".

Dampening

So, if conversion or removal of a barrier are not options, the next option is what we call "dampening". This is where we tackle the barriers that were unable to be either converted to contributors or be removed from the balance entirely. Dampening is the process by which we move the remaining barriers further towards the pivot point, reducing their leverage and hence increasing the chances of reaching the tipping point.

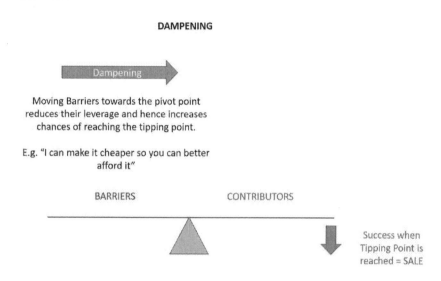

DAMPENING

Moving Barriers towards the pivot point reduces their leverage and hence increases chances of reaching the tipping point.

E.g. "I can make it cheaper so you can better afford it"

BARRIERS   CONTRIBUTORS

Success when
Tipping Point is
reached = SALE

The very simplest example of this would be regarding the price of a product. On the left-hand side, the negative side of the sales balance may sit the price of the product. By reducing the price, you are moving this factor closer towards the pivot point. Once moved, it becomes less of an issue for the customer, less of a barrier that is steering them away from making the purchase. However, there are other ways of adjusting the price, perhaps even without giving away income, to dampen its effect on the customer's purchasing decision.

Dampening The Impact Of Cost

One way of dampening the impact of the cost on the balance, without conceding income, is by restructuring the pricing. You might do this in several ways. By taking the principal sum, and breaking it down into manageable payments, you could still receive the same amount of income and yet the pricing appears far more palatable to the customer. Indeed, it may even be possible to add additional charges, such as interest on the purchase price, but still achieve an element of dampening. Take note of all the relevant regulations regarding pricing and in particular how you have to treat consumers.

It is often the case that a person is prepared to pay more for an item in the long term, providing the monthly payments are more manageable. One only has to look at the development of mobile phone contracts, in order to see this in practice.

As the cost of mobile phones have escalated dramatically, now past the £1,000 mark in order to possess the latest status symbol, the price has moved beyond the immediate purchasing power of many people.

The mobile phone industry has responded to this by breaking down the significant upfront cost into small, manageable, monthly payments. These are paid over an ever-increasing term, but one during which the customer hardly notices the regular small monthly payment leaving their bank account. A few years ago, you may have paid off the cost of your new upgraded mobile phone over the course of two years, now this may have been extended to 3 years, in order to keep the monthly payments down, and at a manageable level, whilst still covering the cost.

The IT sector is another segment where we see a similar type of approach. Buying a new computer system for an office can be an expensive purchase. Once you tally up the cost of PCs, servers and the support time required to set it all up, it can come to a significant sum. An upfront cost of many thousands of pounds can be a significant barrier to a potential customer.

Again, the approach taken by some IT companies is often to form partnerships with leasing and hire purchase companies. These financiers will cover the cost upfront (so the IT company gets paid immediately) and the financier then allows the customer to make manageable monthly payments, over an extended period. Once again, this apparent concession comes at the cost of interest charged over the life of the finance agreement which can be a source of additional income. However, it presents the customer with a way of making a big capital expenditure affordable, so they are willing to pay the additional cost of the interest to overcome the cash flow problem.

Car finance, now common place, is similar. Not only does the buyer benefit from the purchase being broken down into small monthly payments but a significant proportion of the cost may be deferred as a "balloon payment". This is a large chunk of the value that is only due at the end of the finance contract at which point many buyers are encouraged to take a new car and refinance all over again. Deferring this large part of the purchase cost enables the monthly payments to be set much lower, appealing to a much greater number of purchasers.

One last example of restructuring pricing, affects sectors such as the sale of marketing data and the use of stock images for website. In these cases, some sellers have addressed the issue of having to charge large fees for what they are providing by offering a subscription-based model.

This means that the customer is paying a regular subscription, on an indefinite basis, to continue to maintain their license to use the product. In the long term, the amount paid for such a licence could dramatically exceed the value of the product that has actually been used by the customer, but once again the customer is happy to pay a small regular charge when a large single fee may have been seen as a significant barrier.

These are just a few examples of strategies to restructure pricing in a way that dampens its impact on the sales balance, but they might give you some ideas about how you can address the issue of pricing, as it affects your customers.

Would it surprise you if I said your success in dampening the impact of cost depends on whom in the organisation you are talking to? The entrepreneur wants to "make it good and make it gone" so, to appeal to the dynamic called "satisficing", they are more likely to accept the first practical solution that presents itself, and its price.

Not so the finance manager. They may be more data rational. They may be more focused on cost rather than value. They might be the last person you have to negotiate with after the business owner has accepted your quote. They may want to drive down these costs because that's their job. If you have to pitch to someone who holds the purse strings you may want to try giving them a price that is not rounded, especially if you are selling a service, maybe for a monthly price. It's not £300 per month, it's not £295 (they will see straight through that). Its £293.50 but you can give them a discount of 3.25% Your price is the result of a careful consideration of figures and margins by your own finance managers. If they want you to make it cheaper, ask them what price they had in mind. They may not be able to tell you, just that it should be less (so they can make more profit).

Consider that if you keep agreeing to further discount the price, the other person may just keep on asking until they reach the point where you won't agree to go lower. Say you will have to go back and run all your costings again. Or better still, tell them that it can't be done for less and which aspects of the service would they like you to cross out (they may not be able to tell you) and make sure you withdraw the offer of the discount at that point, as you have stopped negotiating. Your price was a fair one and if they don't want it, what's the point of offering a discount? It no longer applies if they want to reduce the price. Make sure they understand this isn't a game, don't be petulant, just realistic. You haven't deliberately inflated the price to be beaten down, or where does it stop? You are running a business too, you deliver a quality service, you have quoted what the customer said he wanted. You may have to walk away.

In conclusion, appeal to the finance manager's reliance on the granularity of costs and the sheer hard work that has gone into your quotation. They will be more likely to accept your price and be happy they got that discount, especially after you withdrew it.[vi]

Additions

Now turning to the positive, right hand side of the sales balance where the contributors sit. We can make further adjustments to these weights, to move the balance towards its tipping point.

Converting Inert Factors Into Contributors

The reason for jotting the inert factors down as described previously, is that you might be missing an opportunity. Taking the previous example, the fact that the customer plays golf could be an opportunity for you to add motivation towards making the sale. Perhaps, inviting the prospect out for a game of golf could build the relationship with them, and place more motivation on the positive side of the balance, moving the balance towards its tipping point.

There are several aspects at play here. Firstly, you might potentially improve the relationship between yourself and the customer buying engaging in such a social activity. This could increase the amount that they like you and this could encourage them towards purchasing from you.

Secondly, if you were to offer the customer something, such as a round of golf, they may feel an element of obligation towards you. This could place further weight on the positive side of the sales balance, moving it further towards its tipping point. This concept is based on the idea that people like to respond in kind when they feel obliged. When someone gives you something, you feel in their debt and there is an element of obligation to respond to that action. Okay, this might not be sufficient to tip the balance in every case, but this could be that tiny additional weight that pushes the balance towards the sale.

But how do you apply this type of thinking in a situation where we are in lockdown or unable to have that personal F2F contact with customers? Well, you may not be able to invite a customer out for a round of golf, but there are other ways of invoking the same feeling of indebtedness. For example, something simple like forwarding them an article relating to golf, because you think it might be of interest to them. Something like this could contribute towards them feeling warmer towards you and to some extent, in your debt. These weights may have some positive effect, moving the sales balance towards the sale.

Whilst the concept of converting inert factors into contributors is certainly something that could contribute towards moving the balance, it might not be the simplest way of influencing the sales situation and moving the balance towards the tipping point.

We have seen how small changes can cause the balance to tip, but as a general rule, we should be looking for heavyweight contributors to move the positive side of the balance downwards.

Additions are weights that can be added to the positive side of the sales balance, in order to move you towards the tipping point.

This is demonstrated in the following diagram:

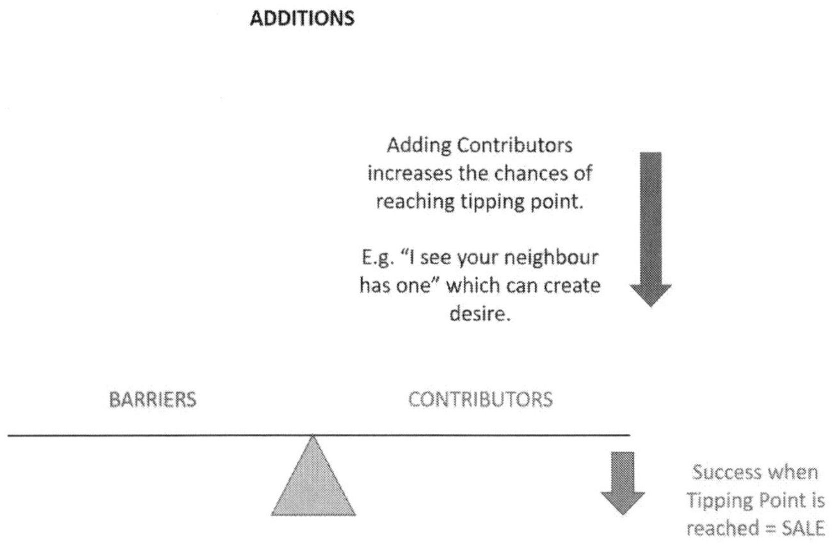

ADDITIONS

Adding Contributors
increases the chances of
reaching tipping point.

E.g. "I see your neighbour
has one" which can create
desire.

BARRIERS   CONTRIBUTORS

Success when
Tipping Point is
reached = SALE

A simple example could be selling a computer software system to a customer, using a phrase such as "I see that your competitor uses a similar system". This can create more desire on the part of the customer, who is influenced in several ways.

Firstly, there may be a desire to keep up with their competitors, not wishing to be left behind. Secondly, this type of phrase also invokes that desire to follow the behaviours of others. As a rule, humans are programmed to feel comfortable copying what they see other humans doing successfully – it's a safety mechanism. You only need stand in the street and point, and you will notice that others will start to look to see what you are pointing at. People follow others.

In its simplest form as applied to sales, this is the situation where a customer sees other customers purchasing, and then decides to follow "the crowd" and purchase themselves. This is why it is such an influential action when you share case studies regarding other customers where you have sold successfully.

Numerous online customer review sites have sprung up to leverage this facet of human behaviour. People like to follow where other people have already gone as there is safety in numbers.

If you are not already collecting customer reviews, it is something that you should consider. Increasingly customer practice is to conduct an internet search to see what other people think of a potential supplier. You can get out ahead of that type of searching by ensuring that you encourage satisfied customers to provide you with review. If you don't, you run the risk that only the minority of dissatisfied customers will take the time to post reviews about you online. There are plenty of services that will interview customers for you, and post reviews e.g. Trustpilot. Or there are sites that offer a mechanism for customers to post reviews independently e.g. Google. Alternatively, you could request the reviews from customers yourself, and post the reviews on your website. However, be aware that customers may think that you have introduced a bias if you are not using an independent service or platform.

Another way of using the power of safety in numbers is to provide customers with case studies, that demonstrate how other customers like them have benefitted from using your offerings. When a customer reads a case study regarding other customers that they feel are like them, it reinforces this aspect. The idea is that because somebody else has already purchased, therefore it must be something positive and safe to do. This is the classic sales behaviour that you see on market stalls. Once one person purchases, the crowd follows as they think "if somebody else wants it then it must be good!".[vii]

So going back to the example phrase that I used above, "I see that your competitor uses a similar system", you are adding a further weight to the positive side of the sales balance. The fact that there is a pre-existing herd mentality to be followed, and that there is a desire to keep pace with their competitors, adds downward force to the positive side of the sales balance.

Where you place this weight along the positive side of the balance, depends upon the amount of leverage that you feel it has. In some cases, it may be highly compelling to see a competitor using a particular system. However, in other situations, somebody that is keen on swimming against the tide, may not find this such a motivating force. Therefore, you will need to place the weight along the sales balance, according to where you judge its degree of leverage to be.

Whilst there is no limitation to the number of items that you can add to the balance, one always needs to be mindful about avoiding overkill. More about that later.

"People like to follow where other people have already gone – there is a safety in numbers."

Yes, Glenn, but remember sometimes people want to stand out from the crowd too – no-one said this was easy!

Checkpoint Summary

1) The weight of all factors is not equal, look for the heaviest weights.

2) Even the smallest 1g weight can tip the balance if it is at the point of equilibrium.

3) Conversions – turning barriers into contributors (the art of sales alchemy).

4) Removals – taking barriers away.

5) Dampening – reducing the effect of barriers that cannot be removed.

6) Additions - can you add further contributors to the balance?

Amplifications & Increasing Leverage

Next, we look at how to amplify the effect of the contributors that are sitting on the positive side of the sales balance. Amplification is achieved by moving the contributors away from the pivot point of the sales balance, towards the right-hand end of the balance. The further that they get away from the pivot point, the more leverage they have and hence the more force they exert on the balance. The more force they exert, the more likely a tipping point is to be reached.

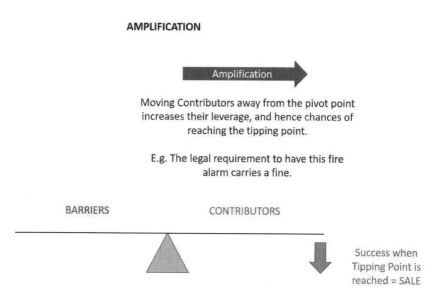

AMPLIFICATION

Amplification ➤

Moving Contributors away from the pivot point increases their leverage, and hence chances of reaching the tipping point.

E.g. The legal requirement to have this fire alarm carries a fine.

BARRIERS   CONTRIBUTORS

Success when Tipping Point is reached = SALE

How do you amplify a contributor? A simple example could be that "gaining a discount" sits on the positive side of the sales balance, near the pivot point as the customer is unlikely to be concerned about a few percentage points off the sale price. It is a positive benefit, but the amount of the benefit is relatively small, hence it does not exert a huge force on the positive side of the balance. You may be able to affect that.

As an example, if you were to dramatically increase the amount of the discount, that factor could be moved significantly towards the right-hand side of the balance, exerting significantly more force, propelling the balance towards the tipping point. Even more force and leverage may be applied by making the discount time bound. If the availability of a discount expires after a certain time, the customer may feel more strongly compelled to move towards agreeing the sale as quickly as possible. Therefore, by time boxing a discount, you could amplify its effect on the positive side of the sales balance.

Be careful, tactics such as placing a timeframe on the uptake of a discount, will not always be positively received. In some cases, a customer may perceive this as an undue pressure, and this could even act as a demotivating factor, moving what was a contributor, towards the opposite side of the sales balance. This of course is exactly the opposite of the adjustment that you are trying to make. Having said that, act reasonably and it is likely to be a positive encouraging influence upon your customer. *It would normally be considered reasonable to present a time limited offer by appealing to the Fear Of Missing Out that nearly all of us feel.*

Avoiding Overkill

This is a warning to anyone who blindly follows the process with no limitation on the number of issues addressed, or the number of adjustments made. You can have too much of a good thing. The idea of a salesperson relentlessly hammering home a list of benefits may do more to detract from making a sale, than it will to encourage it.

It is a delicate finesse, you need to do just enough to reach the tipping point, and achieve your objective, without overkill. You also need to be able to identify the point at which you need to pull back from pressing the customer in order to still retain the possibility that you could sell to them another day.

Techniques such as relentless objection handling can be off putting customers, painting them into a corner to the point that they end up pitted against you. This can happen with telesales calls. Asking the customer "may I ask why not" can be invaluable in surfacing hidden barriers, but after a pushy salesperson repeats that question numerous times, you feel that they are not respecting what you may believe are very reasonable objections.

It is a difficult balance to strike. Sales can often be achieved by identifying and managing objections, but you have to know where to draw the line.

Most people can tell when a customer is starting to become frustrated at the perceived "pressure" that is being applied by the salesperson. You need to give it your best shot, but at the same time don't press too hard. At that moment when you have reached that point, one option is to change tack and "reverse momentum", there is more about that later.

Checkpoint Summary

1) Amplifications – making contributors have more effect.

2) Avoid overkill – don't keep reciting the benefits, adding weights or engaging in relentless objection handling.

Some More Sales Wisdom

These are a few more pieces of sales wisdom that might help you be more successful.

The Dangers Of Selling On Price

It is worth saying something about the dangers of selling on price, where your approach is overly focused on the pricing of the product. It may seem like the easiest, most straightforward approach but it can lead you to sell yourself short. If you can create a perception of value in your customer's mind, the issue of price is less of a concern – they may pay more. If all you do is focus on the price, you diminish your offering, as that is the only aspect that they focus upon.

I worked with a salesperson that primarily focused on the price of the product. On average that person generated less revenue than those that focused on other aspects. If your go to strategy is to discount the pricing, there is only one way to go – down! Consider the other side of the sales balance, the weight of the contributors. Perhaps think about how you can enhance and demonstrate those, rather than heading straight to the discount bargain basement of price.

Do Not Start At Rock Bottom

Leading on from my comments about pricing, a quick word about how you introduce price (again this could fill another book!). If you have any authority to adjust pricing, I suggest that you never open a negotiation at your "rock bottom price".

Customers often like to feel a victory in having negotiated a discount. If you start at rock bottom pricing, again you have nowhere to go but down. By starting off at your target price (a margin above rock bottom), and deciding the point at which you would walk away from the sale (rock bottom), you can attempt to achieve a marginal improvement upon the minimum that you can accept, and even allow the customer a "victory" in the process. This type of concession can be made in return for something that may be of more value to you. For example, in the finance sector, having a customer commit to a 12-month contract, albeit at a slightly discounted price, may be more attractive than a one-month commitment at the full rate. These items can be balanced off against one another, for example, price against commitment period or service level against price.

Another factor at play is the psychology of choice when making comparisons with competitors. To get this part right you must know your competitors extremely well and decide where your price is in relation to theirs.

Consider four companies: A, B, C, D selling a similar product. A is £500, B is £300, C is £250, and D is £100.

Let's make it visual as it has more impact:

£500   A
£450
£400
£350
£300   B
£250   C
£200
£150
£100   D

You are now thinking (without thinking) that the correct price for this product is where B and C are. You are also thinking "Why is A so expensive?" and you are already thinking that if you were to let A sell to you, you would hear all about superior build quality, finish, durability etc.

You are also thinking "Why is D so cheap?" it must be rubbish, or worse, it's not a genuine price. There will be hidden extras to bump you up nearer to B and C (this is known as "lowballing" and it is widely hated).

Of course, there are people who always want the cheapest or the most expensive. You must uncover those people as quickly as you can and act accordingly, depending on the features of your own business and its products and services. But the majority will go through the thought process I've just described. B and C will close most deals and should only have to compete against each other. This dampens the weight with the price label. Consider how to be more successful if you are like B or C.

That example also reminds me of the "three box choice" approach to presenting your offering to customers. When offering any product or service you can package it up into three boxes, one smaller, one medium and one large. Even if it's not literally in a box, the methodology can be applied e.g. to services, the large box equivalent for a service may be with all the additional extras added in.

So, you then present the three boxes to the customer. The medium box is the one that you really expect them to buy, the larger box a few might buy (some people always want the best as Mike said above). The smallest box also presents a budget option, which may appeal to some customers that wouldn't have otherwise purchased anything.

However, the other benefit of presenting your offering in this way is that it positions the normal service (the medium box) as a cut above the basic, smallest box. This lends it value. The buyer is no longer choosing the normal service, it's perceived as an enhanced version. Many people don't want to be seen to be choosing the cheapest option – you only have to see how people choose wine at a restaurant to see this in practice. A colleague once told me he always selected the next to lowest cost bottle from any wine list, so as to not appear to his girlfriend that he was buying the cheapest!

One Size Doesn't Always Fit All

Customer are all individual, and although many business models rely upon the concept of mass market supply, most people prefer to feel like an individual customer, whose needs are being taking into consideration.

Many years ago, I was approached by a double-glazing salesman who was offering 5 windows at a fixed price, I think it was £1,400 at the time. Whatever I asked, he came back to his "one size fits all" options of 5 windows for £1,400. I did not buy because I had 6 windows. However, I ended up spending significantly more, over £2,000 because I found another salesperson that listened to exactly what I wanted and tailored everything to my needs.

In general terms, you will be best served by listening to your customers. Attentively identifying their needs and selling to those needs. If they mention that they need to re-glaze their whole house – ask how many windows![viii]

Decision Bias

Generally, people would rather have certainty ahead of probability. Typically, people will take greater risks to avoid losses than to achieve gains. To illustrate: if I was giving you investment advice on £1,000 and told you that you have a 100% chance your return is £1,100 but a 95% chance your return is £1,150 (with a 5% chance you might lose all your £1000), almost everyone would take the £1,100.

If I flip that on its head and told you that, in a weak market where asset values are falling rapidly, you have a 95% chance of losing all your £1,000 investment (meaning there is a 5% you would keep it) or a 100% chance of losing £950, almost everyone would opt for the first one.

You can appeal to your customers' loss aversion by making their decision to buy from you biased not towards what they will get if they go ahead with your proposal, but what they will lose if they don't.

Don't confuse this with being negative or spreading fear. You need to raise (or better, reflect) the legitimate business concerns that your customer has that can be solved by your product or service. This would be a good time to put this book down and capture a few of your own ideas, relevant to you, that you can refer to later. Just one example question, to ask your customers, to get you thinking: "how much business have you turned away already because you didn't have a solution like mine?".[ix]

Checkpoint Summary

1) Selling on price alone is best avoided, and don't open negotiations with your rock bottom price.

2) Consider how you present options in the light of the psychology of choice.

3) One size doesn't always fit all.

4) Avoiding losses is often a more powerful driver than achieving gains.

Defusing Ticking Timebombs

Sometime there will be a barrier that you are aware of, but perhaps the customer has not mentioned. Maybe it is something that you are worried about them focusing on, that you see it as a point of weakness in your position. These are "ticking timebombs", they are likely to blow up the deal at any given point, especially if you don't get out in front of it and defuse that bomb before it explodes. The temptation is always to avoid them, but you may well be better served addressing them upfront so that you control their impact.

These are the potential barriers that you spend the negotiation worrying will come up. This could be something like a product limitation or a piece of bad press. It could be something simpler, like the fact that you are a small company tendering for a job that might typically be serviced by much larger firms.

Generally, you are better off defusing these timebombs early on, even if the customer has not noticed, or mentioned them. That way you continue to control the way the sales negotiation unfolds, rather than risking losing control, and it being derailed when that issue is placed on the table at a more critical point. If you choose to tackle the timebombs at a point you decide, you can do so in a way that both defuses the issue and creates a feeling of improved trust (a critical part of relationship building) on the part of your customer. If you are "upfront" about a limitation and put that on the table, a customer may assume you have nothing to hide and are treating them honestly. If they "catch you out" later in the negotiation, it may create a suspicion that you are not revealing something else – regardless of the truth.

In the example above of the small company tendering for a larger contract, mentioning that upfront, and perhaps explaining the benefits of a smaller firm in terms of flexibility, service, and responsiveness, could be all that is required. In this way, you might even stand a chance of converting a barrier into a positive contributor. Dealing with a small company could mean better service.

Sometimes, the best way to diffuse the bombs is to list that you know what they are and where they are. Be careful with this approach as you might end up guessing your prospect's concern, trying to diffuse it, only to find out that they weren't concerned or even aware of it. Imagine that you open the bomb disposal section of the closing meeting with "So let me address the issues that everyone else seems to be talking about, why we got bad review over our previous product.." only to be met with "Oh! Really, I hadn't read that". You're now thinking "Damn! Why did I bring that up?".

If you have been practising those listening skills we have been advocating, you should have a good idea what these barriers are. So, list them. Start with something like: "Can I just say out loud what I sense you are concerned about?" then give them all their negative feedback, or areas where you sensed they were holding out on you.

Be sure to check your understanding by closing this section with "is there anything else?" and that's the call back to handling their objections.

As Glenn says, that way you continue to control the way the sales negotiation unfolds.

Magical Thinking

The most impressive part of selling is when you hear a practiced salesperson come up with a clever way of explaining away an objection, or carving up the pricing, such that they customer's fears are allayed and they purchase.

Take the example of selling a watch. If I asked you to sell me a watch how would you start? Would you explain the benefits of the watch? Maybe you would explain it's made of gold, it's exceptionally reliable? Or would you take the watch, pause, and ask me to tell you the time? At that point, you have created a need for the watch, a feat that epitomises what we mean by magical thinking. Impressive as this seems, this example is a simple example of one of the most influential weights: "short supply". This ploy leverages the concept of short supply, I no longer have a watch to tell the time, so the watch acquires value.

This appears to be "magical thinking", that ability to come up with a great way of explaining something or explaining something away! There is no way to teach this, and to some extent it is a natural gift. However, when you are looking for those "magical arguments", return to the checklist of the most influential weights, as those are likely to be the seeds from which those magical thoughts are grown.

Burn Bridges Or Build For The Future?

I would also like to add a note about the amount of frustration that can arise in any sale process. Often one cannot understand why the other party takes a particular stance.

Sometimes people choose to treat salespeople disrespectfully and this can create frustration. In situations where that frustration builds into anger, the temptation to "vent your spleen" and let the customer know exactly what you think, can be almost overwhelming. At that point there is a simple decision to be made – burn your bridges with the customer or try to retain them as a potential future customer?

I have had a situation in my own business where our people have been treated badly by outside parties, and they have prepared an angry email or contemplated a spleen venting phone call. I try to ask – where is that going to lead you? Will you get the sale? Probably not, and in the process, you are likely to lose any chance at a future sale. Is it better to bite your tongue and either work towards getting the sale, or keeping the customer as a possible future purchaser? Personally, I tend to take the later approach and focus on getting the result, rather than satisfying my need to express my outrage, and risk losing the sale altogether. People can let you down, and some can be downright misleading, regrettably in sales that comes with the territory.[x]

Injecting Momentum If Negotiations Stall

It sometimes happens that sales negotiations will reach a point where forward momentum starts to be lost, perhaps you get bogged down with a particular issue that appears unable to be resolved. In such situations it can be useful to have a few techniques to inject momentum back into the negotiations.

Parking An Item

Sometimes a useful technique is to park a difficult item. For instance, this could be useful if you have been haggling about price for a period and you are not really getting towards a conclusion.

It is often price that is the most difficult issue and this technique allows you to sidestep that to solve any other objections. At that point, you might suggest "OK, let's park price for moment, is there anything else that is stopping you from purchasing today?". This may elicit other information from the customer, or they might say nothing, in which case you are back to price – but you have gained the assurance that price is the only remaining issue to solve.

This is a good time to talk about an important technique known as "making the deal area smaller" As Glenn says in this section, park an item that you can't agree on. But make sure they understand that this is the only thing you are coming back to. Making the deal area smaller is a technique that says first: what's important to you? Can you rank these? Can you tell me what's the most important? Ok so if I concede your number one and two, the other point belongs to me. We can't negotiate on everything. So, let's focus in on those areas of the deal where I might be able to get close to you. This is also called the "Zone of Potential Agreement". It forces the customer to think about the things they can have, and what they must give up. Put another way, you are not letting them add or subtract all the weights, move them around, control how the balance works. You make a concession as a trade for the others staying where they are, or even moving in your favour.

Conditional Close

If there are other items to address, you can now tackle those and reach a point where you only have a single barrier left preventing the sale (in my example it is the price). At that point you might offer a conditional close such as "if I can do X on that issue, can we agree the sale now?". This is conditional in that the customer is committing to a course of events whereby if you solve one final issue, and they have already committed to purchase.

As we have said previously, once a customer has agreed to make a purchase (in this case a conditional purchase), they are most likely to carry through on their commitment, as they feel the weight of their obligation, rather than throwing up more barriers for you to address.

In this scenario, you have also made your offer to "do X on that issue" conditional on the purchase. This means that if the customer does throw up another barrier, you have not already made that concession.

The conditional close is an important subtlety in the phrasing that you choose. You need to be careful not to grant the concession, without getting the customer's commitment in return. For instance, if you were to simply say, "OK I will reduce the cost by £50, do we have a deal?", the customer can say "no". At that point you have already put the reduction on the table such that the customer might then say "OK, I will take the £50 reduction you are offering but I also need X". By phrasing your concession as a conditional close you are removing that possibility – they only get the reduction if they agree the sale today.

Introducing New Momentum

If you have been describing the benefits, or you have been handling objections, and you have reached that point at which the customer is beginning to become resistant – showing signs that you are approaching "overkill", you might try something completely different.

For example, you could be honest, acknowledge that you don't seem to be getting anywhere, ask them what they think. Or you might suggest that you and "put a pin" in the conversation and postpone it for another day.

In this way, you may still have a shot at the sale later, rather than losing the prospect completely. There is a similar technique in martial arts. When fighting a bigger opponent, you can reach an impasse, where no matter how much force you exert, they will not move. By rapidly reversing your momentum, for example changing from a push to a pull, your opponent can be unprepared for the change and may be thrown off balance so that momentum is reintroduced. With this technique you may be able to achieve movement where previously there was none.

I want to make another similar point here, about how you can create momentum when the process appears to be stuck. Asking a question such as "what would make you buy today?", can sometimes be helpful in surfacing the primary issues that are in the customer's thoughts – identifying the heaviest weights. You don't have to yield to their demands, instead you might choose to respond with a conditional close such as "OK, so if I agree to do X, will you agree to sign up today?".

A Second Bite Of The Cherry?

There is no shame in marking a prospect forward, retaining the chance that you might sell to them another day. As we described previously, you cannot close every sale, but circumstances do change over time. Something that might not have been quite right for a prospect one day maybe the perfect solution the next. Keeping the dialogue open can result in a "second bite of the cherry" in some cases.

When I started my business, I came across an accountant who was introduced through an associate of ours. It was a short meeting, we were impressed with him, but we had accountants in place at the time. He added us to his email mailing list, and over the course of the next seven years we received regular but infrequent emails from his accountancy practice, updating us about clients they had helped, helpful tips etc.

After that seven year period had elapsed, our circumstances had changed. We no longer felt that the large firm that we were using fitted our needs as well as they had initially. So, we were on the lookout for a smaller, more local accounting practice. I contacted the accountant who had been keeping in contact over the last seven years, and we moved to his practice.

Now if seven years earlier, that same accountant had relentlessly pursued me, citing all the benefits of moving to his practice and belittling my objections, we would probably have parted ways there and then and never got in contact again. He would have lost the potential for the future sale that he made several years later. Also, the cost to that accountant of adding an additional person to his existing email newsletter list was probably almost non-existent.

The moral of the story is that you can live to fight another day. It is better to have the potential of a future sale, rather than have lost the prospect completely today.

This brings us to ways in which you can and sow the seeds in the in "garden" that will yield your future sales. This is how you develop an ongoing sales pipeline and become a next level performer.

Building Your Future Pipeline

It is widely believed that prospective customers are likely to need to have multiple interactions with a brand before they buy, and that also applies to purchasing via a website. On the first pass, you may make some sales, but you will not make all of them. By building a pipeline for future sales, you keep the prospects "in play" such that when their circumstances change, or their feeling for you (or your brand) grows, they may go on to buy from you.

You can do this by keeping yourself at "front of mind". There are lots of ways of doing this, the key is to make the interaction genuine rather than appearing stilted and fake.

In our finance brokerage business, we run an email magazine, which is sent out to customers every month. Our database has been built over years of interacting with thousands of prospects that have had some level of interest in the products that we sell. Many of them did not buy initially but on average we receive a few reignited enquiries every month.

Rather than just endlessly ramming our products down the throat of our clients, we try to add some value within the magazine. In our case, we include articles about business growth, latest industry developments, and success stories from other client situations. Our hope is that some prospects will look at the occasional article and it keeps our name in their mind. This type of long-term interaction also builds an association with your brand, for your prospective customers. You don't need to be face-to-face with someone in order to build this kind of connection – and it doesn't need to have a high cost for each prospect that you add to an established mechanism, such as an email newsletter. I hope that it goes without saying that you need to ensure that you have met the data protection requirements in respect of consent, to add a customer to any form of mailing list.

It is useful to have an underlying message that runs through all the communications that you have with prospective clients. In the case of our finance magazine, the underlying message is that we want to share ideas about how to grow your business and part of the support available to do that is the finance facilities that we arrange. It is most effective if you have some value that you are adding, that benefits the customer, rather than just pushing your products. For example, you could try providing relevant updates are going to be of use to the types of customers that you deal with.

As with all aspects of sales it's important not to overdo it. The regularity with which you contact prospects needs to be appropriate. We send out our magazine monthly, which seemed to us, a reasonable period. Others send out weekly or even daily updates, but in my opinion, those sometimes become annoying, unless the information contained in them is truly of high value to the prospects. I would suggest that you aim to remain well below that threshold of tolerance.

In my opinion, you build a stronger connection with customers if you do not focus on selling to them, but on trying to help and support them. This comes back to the idea that you do not place yourself as an adversary, someone trying to sell to the customer, but as a colleague trying to support them with their purchase. You can go even further, and for example, see yourself as supporting them in growing their business.

However, it is not just about sending out emails, magazines, and newsletters to prospective customers. You can use much more personal approach is, whereby you either call or email prospects on a regular basis, to maintain contact. Again, the key to this is how you position your reason for maintaining contact. It is a delicate balance to remain seen as having a genuine interest, rather than just thinking of making your sale.

This is why, a lot of corporate organisations use an alternative premise in order to maintain contact with prospects or introducers of prospects. In the finance sector, that can include taking customers and introducers to sports events or arranging days out. But now that the world has changed, these practices will need to adapt in to remain of value. This may lead you to consider how you can achieve the same result, without needing face-to-face networking opportunities.

We have seen several approaches develop. There has been a dramatic rise in the number of online webinars. A webinar is an online meeting between multiple prospective connections, and the person that is delivering the webinar. Typically, it will be based around a subject that is allied to the product and service offerings of the host organisation. However, that subject matter can still be addressed with a degree of latitude. Many businesses may be interested in subjects that are not related to your product set, but in hosting such a webinar, you may still be gaining access to prospective customers, and building trust in you and your organisation. You might consider doing this in conjunction with another non-competing business that shares a similar target customer base.

Most businesses have untapped resources within their teams that could be turned into useful free resources, shared with customers and prospective customers, perhaps in a webinar format. Other methods of achieving a similar result are to offer such information via other media. This could include for example, providing online videos via YouTube, to share and disseminate useful information that is allied to the type of products that you are providing.

I would also like to add a note about working smarter, rather than harder. If you are in a sales environment where you must identify your own enquiries, it can be tough to build your pipeline. What about getting other people to do it for you? Developing introducers, rather than end users, can be a more efficient way of spending your time. One introducer can potentially provide you with numerous new enquiries. This may justify any additional cost of acquisition due to paying commission or offering a similar incentive.

The same approach may be possible with your existing customers. If you already have customers that have purchased from you, can you mine them for introductions to similar businesses that they know? This is a powerful technique in that it combines the warmth of an introduction via a party that is already known to the new prospect with the endorsement that comes from the introducing customer, that has already used your offering.

You might argue that introducers are not commonplace within your sector. That could be an advantage. Look for parties that don't have a conflict of interest with you but may share a common customer base. For example, in business finance it is common for financiers to connect with accountants. The accountants often do not offer finance, but they deal with the same customers as the finance companies, and they are in a unique position to introduce customers for finance. You may be able to save yourself a lot of time, effort, and money by developing a few introducers, rather than trying to target just end users for your products or services.

Checkpoint Summary

1) Defuse any "ticking time-bombs" early on e.g. obvious issues.

2) Magical thinking often comes from key motivational forces e.g. short supply, endorsement and safety in numbers.

3) Practice techniques for injecting momentum, if negotiations stall.

4) Don't burn bridges with customers – maintain a low cost/effort follow up process.

5) Work smart and build an introducer network if possible.

How To Move Towards The Tipping Point

So, we have a framework into which we can fit any sales situation, we can identify the forces that are in play and we have a way of prioritising which adjustments to make in order to reach the tipping point and make the sale.

There is also more to say about how you make those adjustments. This encompasses all the sales techniques that address how to close the sale, as quickly as possible.

We had a long discussion in the run up to writing this book, about which was the more powerful force, fear or desire? Is it more expedient to play on the customers fears, or to appeal to their desires? Why do you have to make a choice between the two? Appeal to both at the same time to maximise your ability to get the sales balance tipping towards closing the sale.

This brings us to an important question – how do you close the sale?

Objection Handling

We have already established that in "overkill" is not a good idea. You cannot continue to challenge every barrier that the customer puts forward, without having a negative effect on your chances of making the sale. However, an element of objection handling is an essential part of the process of affecting the sales balance.

There is a place for the "pre-handling" of objections that you can tackle even prior to interaction with the customer.

If you have already developed and populated your sales balance, in advance of the interaction with the customer, to the point that you understand what some of the barriers may be. You can pre-handle some of those objections in the material that you provide to your customers. For example, if one of the barriers may be the lack of trust in your business, as you are unknown to the customer, you may choose to emphasise memberships that you have two relevant bodies or other forms of endorsements from parties that the customer will recognise. By identifying these barriers in advance, and pre-handling them you can remove them from the negative side of the sales balance before the interaction has begun.

When dealing with objections, follow the same system as we set out previously step-by-step: 1) Can you convert the barrier into a contributor? 2) Can you remove it altogether? 3) Can you dampen its leverage by moving it closer to the pivot point.

So that deals with as many of the barriers as possible, in advance of interaction with the customer. The opportunity when you are speaking to a customer is to dig further and try and see if there are any further barriers to completing the sale. You might do this by asking a simple, open ended questions such as "May I ask why?" in response to any objection that the customer puts forward.

If you are trying to sell to a customer that already uses the products or services of one of your competitors, another simple approach to surface the weights that are in play is to ask "what could be improved about the product that you already have?".

This type of questioning will allow you to reveal the customer's needs and you can then sell to the gaps between what the customer needs, and what your competitors are already providing. It's an open question again, but it also has an inbuilt assumption – that there will be something that can be improved. This is another important psychological technique. If you build assumptions into a question the customer will be likely to accept them. Asked simply "if there is anything that could be improved", most people may answer "no". Asked "what can be improved?" more people will respond with something, and every response gives you something to work with, a gap to fill.

Changing The Game

I wanted to mention something about how you might deal with difficult situations, where you are being forced to operate in a way that you are not happy with. For example, sometimes prospective customers will say "look, just give me your best price". Often, they are looking to boil the decision down to something simple, like price (in this example), and/or they are trying to neutralise all other sales techniques that they fear exist only to make them purchase.

Unfortunately, this type of approach throws the baby out with the bath water. Yes, it neutralises the techniques of unscrupulous salespeople, but it also takes out everything else – all the benefits that can be offered by a well-trained sales representative who sees their role as helping the customer make the best purchasing decision. You must decide how you want to respond in those situations, sure you could just give them the price and hope that you compare well. Or, you could be a little more innovative and try to change the game. For example, you could say "I can see you like to get straight to the point. I am the same. My concern is that this type of purchase is risky if the decision is only based on price. I would be happy to review the offers and tell you the pros and cons of each after you have got all the quotes in?".

It may be possible to use an alternative approach like this to step outside of the constraints that are being placed upon you. In the above example, you are offering a free service (to review the quotes), you are setting yourself up as an expert adviser, rather than a salesperson, and you are asking the customer to commit to giving you a final crack at the situation. You don't necessarily have to agree to every request. You have also subtly sowed seeds of doubt over making decisions purely on price. It won't be applicable to all situation, but it might help you in some.

Closing Techniques

This is the easiest part to understand and often the hardest to master. How do you ask if it's okay to move ahead? That doesn't just mean asking for the business, but also this works to move people along the sales continuum to get to that point.

There are tons of closing techniques and as many different names for them. I'm going to run through some of the most successful. As I do, you may recognise all of them. You may be using them already, so this will be a refresher. You may do them intuitively without knowing they had a name. Or you may be coming to some for the first time. The important thing is to know they are nearly always used in combination and are rarely used alone.

Practice makes perfect. You need to start to employ this whole process, coupled with the techniques that are about to be laid out, in order to increase your PP. Try to find low risk situations where you can put these methods into practice e.g. discussions with family and friends. Then you can hone your technique, before you apply them to important sales situations.

The Assumptive Close

The phrasing of an assumptive close implies that the customer will want to go ahead with the proposal or with a meeting. Use words that make it seem like the agreement to proceed has already been given.

Don't give the option but proceed as if the decision to buy/to meet has already been made. Remove any conditional words from your communication (shall, maybe, perhaps, could etc.) and replace them with certainties like "will".

My favourite example was in the local garden centre at the end of last summer. Garden chairs were on sale for half price and I was happy to buy some and put them in my garage until next year. I sat in the dark green display version – perfect! But the stock on the shelf were all orange. "Do you have this in green?" I asked an assistant. "I will check the stock room for you: how many do you want?" I was in awe. I never confirmed I wanted to buy but the assumption was that I was going to, it was just a matter of how many. I could have said "Well I'm not sure I'm going to buy any, I'm just enquiring" or similar. Instead I said "Two" and away she went. I stayed put until she came back empty handed saying they were sold out and the next stock would come in next season. A classic assumptive close that deserved a sale!

This is an example of "implied assumption". You don't specifically state the assumption, but it is implied in what you say. A person's brain is sensitive to such nuances in speech. The fact that you imply something is perceived (at some level), and it can influence their actions. By implying that you expect them to purchase, it is then just a case of deciding in what quantity – you have taken the actual purchase decision out of the equation.

Also, in Mike's example, the very act of getting the chairs for the customer places an obligation on the customer to carry out the purchase. Even if you are not physically in front of a customer with a physical product you can employ this approach. For example on the phone you might say "OK, I am just blocking out Friday in my diary for you", once it's done you have provided something and placed an obligation on the client to proceed.

The Alternative Close

This gives the appearance of choice but builds on the assumptive close. This can be helpful to get a virtual meeting for you to make your pitch and close. In that instance always offer two dates and say something like "Monday or Tuesday, which would suit you better?".

Do not give the option to meet or not. Don't ask when a good date would be for them.

Once they have agreed a date, don't keep offering choices like morning or afternoon? 10 am or 11am? as you will diminish the effectiveness of the first question. Send a meeting invite for a meeting. If it's not a good time on that day, repeat the technique: 3pm or 4pm which works best for you? Do not go back to asking them when a good date for them would be.[xi]

By offering just two, alternative options, it increases the likelihood that the prospect will feel limited to just choosing one of those options that you have presented. If you were to ask an open question, such as "would you like to go ahead?", the customer has not been given any options to choose from and may answer the question with "no".

If, as suggested above, you ask "would you like to go ahead on Monday or Tuesday?", you have seeded that question with a presumption that they will choose one or other of the limited number of options that you have presented to them. Psychologically, this affects the person's decision making. When faced with a simple choice of two options, it's more difficult for a person to then choose a third option that was not on the table e.g. replying, "I'm not going to go ahead".

Hurry Up

"Sale must end Monday" We have all heard it, and we've probably all responded to it. It's mostly about price.

This is often combined with others and its most powerful where you must energise a proposal that has ground to a halt. Basically, you are limiting the time available for them to decide. Don't confuse it with "Short Supply". That comes later and appeals more to our fear of missing out or even our desire to have something exclusive.

Hurry Up is a nice way to think of "make up your mind!". Everyone knows about inflation and price rises so make a virtue of honouring a price that maybe has already expired, but only if they agree quickly.

Warm Puppy

Have you ever been to buy a puppy? Hopefully, it was from a reputable breeder. The puppies are not ready to leave their mother and when you enter the room, they rush over to you! You pick one up and you bond with it! It licks you, it wags its tail, you cuddle it, this is the one for you! And during that time the breeder says . . . nothing – they don't have to.

It's hard to find a helpful parallel experience, but think about test driving a new car, or being shown around a flat or house you want to buy, it's the same thing. There is a strong emotional connection and the item you want will sell itself to you. If you are stimulated most by your feelings (rather than sounds or pictures), this one's for you.

It seems like common sense but if a customer walks into a car showroom the salesperson does not rush over and exclaim "It's £56,000!". Most people would turn tail and walk back out. Instead they offer the chance for you to sit in the car, feel the leather seats, and go for a test drive. It is a seduction rather than a race to get to the finish line. Besides which, barriers such as the price, can often be overcome with some well-structured finance.

Take a moment to think about your own product or service and try to find the parallel. If it's a product, can the customer try before they buy? Are they renewing or upgrading and if so, can you remind them of a positive previous experience? You might remember a TV ad for an iPhone where a customer slowly opens the box containing his new phone. It's a hugely tactile experience and we see his delight when he flexes his fingers before sliding the box open and even licking his lips as he peels off the protective screen cover – the iPhone wags its tail!

If it's a service you provide, is there a customer portal or App that you can demonstrate to your prospect? "This is how it will be when we are looking after you" (notice the combination with an Assumptive Close?)

If your service involves an account manager, can you introduce them to the prospect in advance? But be careful to stress your relationship management is cultural. "All of us at my company are like this. Its why we were hired, we all work the same way" (we are all warm puppies!). If it's just you running the company, then you have a head start in this since you are going to give them your personal attention.

Relationship Building

We have already seen a full explanation of this, and how salespeople who relied on relationship building: getting the prospect to like you, will be feeling unempowered and maybe a little vulnerable in the new environment.

But here's a tip: it's not just about the customer liking you that makes them want to buy from you, it's also about them feeling you like them. Find a way of telling them. Try this: "I like working with you". "I enjoyed our meeting". An apparently small acknowledgement can make a big difference.

But if you studied the Ladder of Affirmation, that was discussed previously, you will by now appreciate that the higher you go, the more they customer will feel valued and appreciated and yes, liked.[xii]

Maintaining Direction

Ever wondered why you get asked to sign an offer, to accept indicative terms or tick a box to say you would like to receive emails etc? In the psychology of choice, what looks like a small action can lead to a change in behaviour. People become more obligated to the proposal and are less likely to cancel it because we want to keep our promises and act with integrity.

Its why salespeople celebrate when they get someone to "sign on the dotted line". Customers tend to stick to a proposal that they have agreed in writing. Not only do we say "I gave my word" but we might also say "I signed up for this" when we haven't actually signed anything. It's more a by-word for an indication that we feel obligated and our integrity makes us go through with it. Bear this in mind when asking the customer to confirm they will go ahead with your proposal.

Avoid sounding petulant when reminding the customer they were committed previously: "But you've already signed up for this!" is not as effective as "I have been working towards delivering what you indicated you wanted".

You might only have a verbal agreement. Reminding the customer to maintain their direction is much easier: just say "like we said" or similar.

That type of behaviour also places you on the same side as the customer, helping them fulfil their previously expressed desire, rather than in opposition, trying to make them do something.

Safety In Numbers

Also known as "tried and tested". Its why product and service review websites have taken on so much importance. It's also why you should constantly review and develop your own testimonials.

When talking to a prospect, if you identify a problem they need to overcome, think if your marketing collateral includes a case study that speaks to the issue. "Here's how we solved that exact problem for someone else".

You need to make sure the prospect customer is aware of what you do and ensure they become more interested in taking it further when they see others that you have worked for.

It can be used when you want the customer to move from desire to action. "I sense you are nearly ready to go on this. Would you like to speak with someone who has worked with us already?".

Some of you might be thinking this sounds a little too safe. Why should my customer follow the crowd or even, herd? In that case a better closing technique might be . . .

Limited Supply

Sometimes called the "Fear of Missing Out", Limited Supply is nearly always used with Hurry Up since the latter is the obvious way to avoid the former.

Some people love to be exclusive and when selling to them, your product or service may seem more valuable to them if it is positioned as being rarer. People can be highly motivated if they are concerned about losing something. You might say "We can get started addressing these issues but quite soon the offer will expire/the price will go up/the product will be out of stock". These limitations of supply can have a powerful motivational effect.

Do You Want It Or Don't You?

This is so important, it is the ultimate question, but one that should only be used once all other avenues have been exhausted.

It's the quickest way to move the customer to say yes or no. It's usually the last question and is often called "Asking for the Business". And of course, there are risks associated with using it i.e. losing the whole proposal at that point.[xiii]

If you feel unable to ask the question using those words, try a summary beforehand: "So you said you are ok with the costs/specification/price. I confirmed we can deliver in the timeframe we have already agreed to fulfil this need that your business clearly has. We agreed everything so, I have to ask; what's stopping you?".

Try to get the customer to list their objections, and then you can handle them one by one. This is called what we previous described, Making the Deal Area Smaller. Then ask the question again. And this time you can be brave enough to recognise if you have a NO and move to the next opportunity.

Recap

I want you to see these closes as ways to move the weights, to tip the balance so you make the sale. It is that simple.

They are very often used in combination and maybe adding a "companion" close at the right time will cause the tip you are looking for.

You will need to work on understanding which are appropriate, and which go together. Then develop your own approach and practice it until its natural for you.

If you found yourself thinking "I'm never going to say or use that!" to any of the above, challenge yourself to find a way to do so. Push yourself out of your comfort zone. As is often said "if you do what you've always done, you'll get what you always got". The world has changed. You cannot rely on what you did before.

Checkpoint Summary

1) Use closing techniques to move towards the "tipping point".

2) Assumptive closes: "how many will you take?".

3) Alternative closes: "would you like 2, or 3?".

4) Utilise short supply and/or time limitations.

5) Employ the power of "relationship building" wherever possible.

6) Ultimately: "do you want it, or don't you?".

Lock In The Decision

Even though the sales balance may have tipped in favour of a sale, that is not the time to stop and rest on your laurels. It is the time to lock in that decision, to reduce the chances that the customer will fail to complete the sales process or will withdraw.

Creating Obligation

As we have already mentioned, one inbuilt driver is that people like to maintain their current direction and live up to their obligations. Once we have made up our minds, it is exceedingly difficult to get us to change them. This driver can also be used to your advantage.[xiv]

If someone has already acted in a way that supports a purchase, they are unlikely to want to change direction. If someone agreed to buy over the phone, or have signed an order, they are less likely to reject the product when it arrives. You can even invoke this in the language that you use. For example, using a phrase to a customer such as "as you said earlier . . ." and then stating something that is congruent with the customer making a purchase, reinforces that you are expecting the customer to continue to act in accordance with what they have already said or done. You have created an obligation on the part of the customer.

This could include getting them to sign an order, taking a deposit or more subtle methods of locking in the purchasing decision.

This is shown in the following diagram:

LOCK IN THE DECISION - POST TIPPING POINT

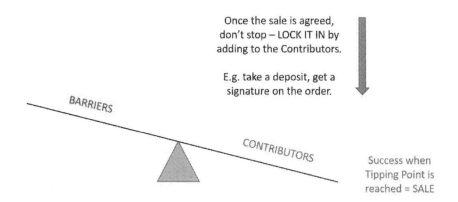

Once the sale is agreed, don't stop – LOCK IT IN by adding to the Contributors.

E.g. take a deposit, get a signature on the order.

BARRIERS

CONTRIBUTORS

Success when Tipping Point is reached = SALE

Have you ever come out of a meeting, or maybe put the phone down and thought "It's in the bag!" only to find the prospect backs out later?

Maybe when they said it, the prospect really did want to proceed. Or maybe there were barriers you hadn't uncovered. Here's a couple of examples of how decisions get locked in, both appeal to what we call "maintaining direction".

After The Sale Decision Confirmation

If you've bought clothes from a certain high street retailer's store, I guarantee you will have heard this: they say it all the time. You will be complimented on your choice of garment when the assistant is bagging it up, just before or maybe after you have already paid. They may say it's a nice colour, or they have also bought one like it, or even that you have made a good choice. Its flattery so that you feel appreciated and liked and so you don't bring it back!

When employing this technique, make your compliment sound natural and play to the weight that tipped the sales balance in favour of the sale. "That's a wise choice, thank you" or "You've got a great deal there!" or " this will be with you in 48 hours and you can put it to work straight away". Find something that is real for your product or service and makes the customer feel they have done the right thing by buying from you.

It's important to avoid what we can call "scripted behaviour" as this can appear disingenuous and has the opposite effect.

Note: I once had a salesperson working for me who was good at this. I was with her on several occasions after the deal had been agreed and even after documents had been signed. Our service was a big commitment and was firmly relationship-based, not transaction-driven. The cost of new client acquisition was high, and this salesperson had studied the instances where new prospects simply never started, even after they had signed and returned documentation. She was convinced the selling wasn't complete until they had commenced.

She positioned herself differently. Now she was the ambassador for the company, always focused on the start date, helping with every step. Nothing was too much trouble. She was the go-between. Now I know what you're thinking: this isn't a very efficient use of her time! The sale was done, hand it over to the onboarding team and move to the next one! Sad to say, the onboarding team lacked sales focus and had a culture where finding a problem (with the transaction) was a success. My salesperson continued to handle objections, smooth the process, hold their hand, and only let the customer go when they were safely on board.

Think about your own business and how many times you have lost a sale you thought (or even boasted) was "in the bag!" I will bet this happens more to relationship-based service sector readers.

That is also a good example of how even putting a signature on a document may not be enough to completely lock in the decision. It is common within the business finance sector for customers to sign agreements, and yet never commence drawing down their facility. Regardless of sector, salespeople need to identify exactly what their objective is. Is it agreeing the sale? Or getting an order signed? Or getting the money in from the sale? Wherever you, or your organisation, draw(s) the line determines how long you should remain involved – guiding the customer to reach the final objective.

Maintaining direction comes into play once you have created an obligation that is felt by the customer. In my training company I always get my customer to sign a works order detailing what we have agreed. The dates for the seminars and workshops maybe months ahead. I want them to see themselves as keeping their promises and behaving honourably because they have given taken on an obligation. I've never had anyone back out once they have got to this point. There is powerful psychology at work here!

So, think about your own product or service: what can you say to endorse the customer's choice, and encourage them to maintain their direction i.e. completing the purchase? Draw attention to the weights that swung the decision in favour of a sale. Maybe reprise those points that drew your attention up front: a call-back to your agenda.

A Simple System

So that has explained our system in quite a bit of detail. What we will do next is to boil this approach down into a simple series of steps that you can follow in any sales situation where you want to influence another person.

This simple flowchart summarises our system:

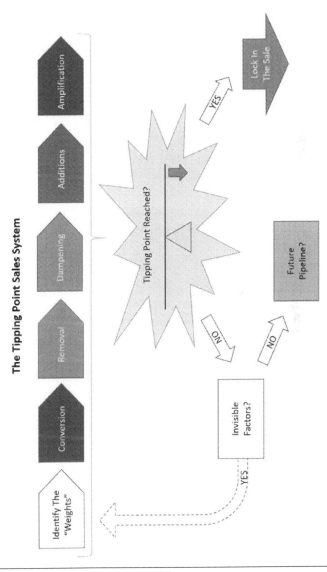

Our system works because of this straightforward process:

Step 1 - IDENTIFY – Identify the weights on the balance using open questions (or by research or by using your intuition). Where are the heaviest weights?

Step 2 - Focus on adjusting the barriers first:

CONVERSION – can you convert the barrier into a contributor?
REMOVAL – can you remove the barrier altogether?
DAMPENING – can you dampen its effect?

Step 3 – Adjust the contributors:

ADDITIONS – Can you add contributors or use inert factors?
AMPLIFICATION – Can you increase the leverage of any contributors?

Step 4 - LOCK IN THE DECISION – When you reach the sale, lock it in! Use Decision Confirmation if possible.

If you are still not at the tipping point, consider:

INVISBLE WEIGHTS – Are there invisible weights at play that you can address?

If you still can't get to the tipping point:

FUTURE PIPELINE – Can you mark it forward for future follow up?

The system is most efficient when you prioritise the "heaviest weights", which have the biggest effect on the balance. In any situation it is wise to check that you are utilising all the weights at your disposal. Can you present a product that appears to be in short supply? Are you able to demonstrate that others have already successfully purchased, or that your product is endorsed by respected third parties? These are likely to have the greatest impact on reaching "tipping point".

Checkpoint Summary

1) Refer to the Tipping Point Sales System diagram and follow the steps for each sale.

2) Lock in the purchasing decision e.g. signing an order or taking a deposit.

Using All The Available Channels

At this point we have given you a system which can be applied to any situation where you are seeking to influence others in a sale negotiation. The system strips back sales processes and techniques to expose the underlying mechanics of what occurs in practice. It leads to a nice simple step by step approach that you can use to maximise the chances of being successful.

The next phase is to look at how you can approach each of the sales channels that are open to you, to maximise your success.

Structuring Your Pitch

With face to face selling becoming more limited, not to mention time consuming and expensive, what alternative sales channels are available to connect with customers? Of course, it depends upon the sector that you operate within, and the nature of your product and services, but there are some obvious candidates.

The obvious replacement for F2F meetings is the use of video conferencing, or even just phone-based meetings. There is plenty of tech booming at present on the back of the surge in video conferencing (VC). Whilst VC gives something more than just voice over the phone, it still falls someway short of what you gain from a F2F meeting. VC can be prone to accidental over talking, awkward pauses and lapses in connectivity – all of which can significantly impact your effectiveness. Even the process of getting everyone onto a VC can be torturous, with accurate timing being of the essence in a way that it just is not for F2F meetings. However, we must work with what we have.

The other positive for VC is that the lockdown has caused its popularity to soar. Whereas it may have been seen as gimmicky pre-lockdown, it has become an essential tool for many businesses that have now successfully trialled it, albeit out of necessity.

When planning a VC interaction with a prospective customer, you should put as much effort into appearance as you would if you were going to meet them F2F. You have an opportunity to "stage the scene". This means carefully choosing the background for the VC, rather than leaving it to chance. You need to choose an area with good lighting for obvious reasons, you can also put some effort into the background in order to begin the process of influencing your prospect.

For example, a view which includes certificates on the wall, could invoke feelings of trust due to the customers perception of you being an expert.

The look and feel of the room is important. It will be the first visual signals that you give your customer. You may choose to include some personal cues within the scene that could potentially open conversations with the prospect. For example, a signed football shirt on the wall of your home office, could lead to prospects asking you about your interest in football. This could be part of relationship building, establishing some mutual ground, and the more the prospect warms to you and trusts you, the more likely the sale becomes.

Also consider the technology available. How good is the camera and microphone on your current laptop or tablet? Consider a separate webcam and microphone. Better yet, get some in-ear headphones so the audio through your speaker doesn't create a feedback loop.

The same goes for your personal appearance and presentation. Unlike making a phone call, with VC, the prospect can see at least some elements of your appearance. Your choices are likely to be driven by the nature of the sector within which you operate. When operating within say finance, we would tend to wear at least a shirt but perhaps a shirt and jacket for a VC call. In other sectors this might not be so critical, but remember that the visual image you are presenting to the customer accounts for a significant proportion of the message that they will be receiving about you.

You can enhance that experience, by presenting a carefully constructed appearance and background setting, in order to evoke helpful thoughts in the mind of the prospect. If a prospect sees you sitting in overly ornate lavish surroundings, this could cause him to question how much you are charging for your services. Similarly, unsightly surroundings could produce a negative perception.

In general terms, do not overengineer this aspect of the VC. Go for a professional background, perhaps including a few visual cues that invoke the idea that you are qualified and perhaps giving away some hints towards a personal interest, to open the possibility of conversation.

Similarly, with your personal appearance, you may not want to appear too formal, but still do not want to come across as if you are sitting on the beach on holiday! Somewhere in the middle is probably a good balance.

It has been very easy during times where people were locked down, to become complacent about your appearance. Again, think carefully about the visual image that you are presenting to your customers.

There are other channels which you might describe as "promotion" either online (web, social media and email based), or offline (traditional paper-based formats). Those in sales can perhaps make more use of these methods as they may have traditionally seen them as the realm of the marketing department. When you are getting less opportunities to get in front of people, it is wise to widen the tools at your disposal and many of these channels are increasingly falling under the remit of the salespeople. For example, many salespeople see social media channels such as LinkedIn and Twitter as increasingly important sources of new enquiries.

Phone & Video Based Selling

Phone selling is almost the same as F2F, and VC is identical - isn't it? Wrong. These are hugely different media, you can almost think of it as trying to speak through a wall, most of what you normally expect to get through to the prospect is lost.

Phones only transmit mid-range frequencies, so they limit tone (over a third of communication if you remember) and there is little transmission of gesture. Therefore, you need to focus on your honing your message and its delivery, to maximise your conversion – which is where there is something we can learn from telemarketers.

The "Lobster Pot"

Fully scripted conversations and responses really don't flow that well when delivered via the telephone or even VC. Having said that, it is useful to have a structure to your interactions with a prospect, based on the system that we have described previously. I tend to create a set of call guidelines which do not prescribe exactly what will be said, there are more of a memoire of useful phrases and objection handling points that can help guide the conversation.

You can apply the techniques which I am going to describe to both cold calling situations, where you don't know the prospect and conversations where you are contacting customers that are already known to you. In all interactions you should retain the sales balance in mind, and work to adjust towards reaching the tipping point.

At the heart of a good set of call guidelines Is the "lobster pot". If you have ever seen how people try to catch lobster, you may be familiar with the structure of a lobster pot. They come in different shapes and sizes, but the key feature that they have in common is that they contain some bait, something to attract the lobster, and have an aperture through which it is easy for the lobster to enter, but it is difficult to exit. Like a one-way valve system.

We can apply the same principle to the development of our call guidelines. We are looking for an opening gambit, to use with the prospect, that welcomes them in, but makes it difficult for them to exit the interaction. For example, if you were selling finance, you might ask a customer "what would you spend an additional £50,000 on? ". The idea of £50K is the bait, but the question is structured so that there is no easy exit. It is difficult to answer this question by just saying I don't want £50,000! As children we are often taught that we must answer questions when asked. Therefore it is ingrained in us that we should do so rather than refusing.

If you were to structure that initial question as "do you want to borrow £50,000", you are likely to have a far greater proportion of prospects simply answering "no"! The lobster pot no longer functions as there is an easy exit. There is a connection here to some of the closing techniques were discussed previously. Remember the Alternative Close where we only offered two choices and implied that one of them would be selected?

So the former question may be our lobster pot opening. It is likely that the customer will feel compelled to answer the question, in some way rather than telling you that they are not interested. At this point you start to extract information about what the customer's needs may be. In very simple terms understand their needs and then sell to those needs, populating the sales balance as you go.

When you were trying to construct your "lobster pot" opening, as in the case above, very small adjustments to the wording can make a big difference to the effectiveness of the question. My £50K question carries the implied assumption that you will have a purpose for the £50K, I'm simply asking you to tell me what that would be.

Once you have your opening, and you start to extract information about the needs of the customer, you can use that to populate the sales balance, and then follow the steps that we have set out above to try and reach the tipping point for that customer.

You can then continue to construct your call guidelines In a similar way to this first step. Try to phrase further questions in a way that they minimise the opportunity for the customer to just say "I'm not interested" and crawl out of the proverbial lobster pot.

When calling a prospect who told you they were not interested then, but maybe in the future, consider structuring your second call questions so you get a "no" as a way to get people into the lobster pot. Salespeople are sometimes taught to get a "yes", and a prospect on their guard will be wary of giving you too many: "you want to save money?" "You want your business to succeed?" "You want to leave your competitors behind, don't you?" I may answer "yes" to all three but now I'm on my guard because your next sentence in going to be ". . . then you really can't afford to live without my . . ." and when I say I can live without it; I am going to sound like I've gone back on what you made me say yes to.

So, you might try asking a question that gets you a no straight away. It's a safe space for the prospect and they might be off guard. Let's say you are in recruitment, called a prospect to see if they had any temporary vacancies and they said, "not right now, maybe later on". When you call them again, try something like "Have you given up looking for temporary staff?". I doubt if they will rush to say "Yes". A natural inclination is to say no, since it sounds like they are saying no to you. But they may have just entered your pot!

Anticipating Barriers

In the sector of corporate finance where we operate, there are relatively few suppliers when compared with other sectors as it is quite a specialist niche. We had a spate of finance prospects where we would open the dialogue with them and get to a point where we talked about starting to make introductions to funders. At this point, the customer would decline as they were already in contact with the funders that we were proposing. As the nature of business finance has got more and more competitive, this has become an increasingly problematic issue. It needed to be addressed, we needed to tackle this barrier before it arose and derailed each sales negotiation.

We wanted to remove as many barriers from the sales balance as we could, pre-interaction with the customer. Now when we are conducting that initial dialogue with the new prospect, once we have identified a need, and overcome any major objections to proceeding, we now ask "Are there any providers that you are already speaking to, or would not wish to hear from?". It is a simple question, but it has saved us an enormous amount of time. It surfaces what are often one of the invisible weights pressing down on the sales balance, working against making the sale. When constructing your call guidelines, think about the similar barriers that you are likely to face, and how you can head off those objections before they even occur.

Checkpoint Summary

1) Consider using more of the available communication channels with customers.

2) Employ "lobster pots" – phrases that solicit positive responses, whilst deterring exits.

3) Anticipate barriers and where possible handle them up front.

Online & Offline Selling

The other channels of communication available in this new scenario, where we are no longer always face-to-face with prospects, include online and off-line media. These could be ways in which you follow up with existing prospects (other than via phone/VC) or ways in which you build your pipeline by generating new enquiries. In some organisations the generation of new enquiries falls to the marketing department and may be outside of the salesperson's remit. However, in others the opposite is true, and of course there are owner managed situations where the owner takes on all roles.

There is a nice simple process flow here though. The generation of new prospects, leading through to the selling process via whatever media are available and then a follow up process for prospects that didn't convert, but may at a later date.

By online we mean anything connected to the Internet. This would include webpages and blog posts, social media, and email contact. Many salespeople use these to build an online presence, become an expert in their field and potentially attract enquiries from prospective customers. Off-line would mean anything that is not related to the Internet. This could include paper-based materials such as brochures and mailings, or other promotion and advertising. The principles of preparing material for any medium are broadly the same. The selection of the medium should be tailored to your target customers, however there is often a cost advantage in using online media rather than having to cover the expense of printing and delivering physical materials.

There is a huge opportunity here to incorporate these media into your sales process, in order to both increase the number of leads that you get, and improve your conversion ratio. Responding to calls for help on social media can be a source of new leads, whilst a regular email newsletter to your existing prospects could be a way of re-engaging with existing prospects that have gone cold. These can be a very low-cost ways of engaging with a large number of ex-prospects and potential prospects. In many cases the biggest investment required will be your time.

The selection of the medium should be driven by which is most appropriate, and accessible, to your prospective customers. An email newsletter will be great for most businesses, but if your target market is the elderly, a paper-based approach is likely to be far more effective at reaching your audience. Whichever medium you select, the overall approach to producing the communication is broadly the same. Always trying to move prospective customers towards a point where the sales balance tips. The first step is often to get them to connect with you, so it is important how you structure your communications, whether it is a social media post, an email or any other material that prospective customers may see.

Structuring Communications

Essentially, there should be three parts to any message:

Attract – Engage – Connect.

So, we will look at each of those component parts, in turn.

Attract

The first part of any message is the "bait" a short compelling headline that attracts a customer to explore further. On a blog post this could be a title, on a social media post it could be the opening sentence, or it could be the heading in an email that you sent to prospects.

The key thing is that that needs to be succinct and compelling. Again, look for those heaviest of weights to apply the maximum leverage. For example: a finance broker may write: "One supplier has just halved their prices". The headline is interesting as it suggests that "half price" may now be possible. It also draws the reader in, as they want to find out which supplier is providing that offer, and this is not revealed in the headline.

Engage

The second part of any communication is to engage the prospect. This is where you provide slightly more material, relaxing the prospect into communication with you, or your brand. This is an opportunity to provide something, even if it is only information, that then sits in the customer's mind as an obligation to return the courtesy and provide something to you (hopefully an enquiry!). Again, don't rush to reveal all the details immediately, you need to strike a balance so that they prospect gets in touch, allowing you to engage your sales skills. You should minimise the information that may discourage enquiries, whist remaining truthful of course, as advertising in the UK is now policed by the Advertising Standards Agency who will take a dim view of misleading or untruthful promotional materials.

Too much detail can put prospects off. You may be able to put all the terms and conditions in a separate document. Engagement is about building the relationship with your customer.

Once again, use the heaviest weights. For example: "XYZ Limited are offering customers 50% off of the normal costs, however you only have until the end of the month to qualify". This statement uses "limited supply" to increase the customer's desire.

Connect

The last part of the communication should be the "call to action" that creates a connection with the prospect. This depends very much on at what stage the customer is (an existing prospect, or a cold lead) but it could be asking them to click through to your website, it could be asking them to complete a contact request form or to call you back. In some cases, it may be completing the sale and taking the money via a card payment. This is the most important part of the communication where you secure the prospect so that either the transaction is completed, or they can be followed up. You need to make this as simple and easy as possible so that it maximises the number of prospects that contact or re-contact you. A simple "get in touch" form may be more attractive than having to fill out a detailed application that requires a lot of information. Every piece of information you ask for, however useful, is one more barrier on the sales balance which may cause the prospect to put off responding.

The call to action also needs to be low risk from the prospect's perspective. If you design a form that asks for too much detailed information, a prospect may be put off, or become cautious about supplying so much data. It is far better to ask for basic information, so that you can then contact them to follow up.

This gives you the chance to invoke "relationship building" as part of your process, tipping the balance further in favour of a sale. By minimising the complexity, and the value, of the information that you are requesting, you are dampening the negative impact of this barrier on the balance. This is an important consideration as we live in times when personal information has become increasingly guarded, and many are wary of providing data even if you have secure protocols in place. It's worth mentioning that simple things, such as adding an Secure Socket Layer (SSL) certificate to a website (this is the secure padlock that appears in your web browser) can add a feeling of security – even if it's not strictly speaking required i.e. you aren't taking customer payments over the internet. Just having that green padlock in the corner may partly alleviate concerns over trusting you and your site.

The subject of generating trust via the web is a huge issue. Most people are aware of the ever-increasing number of fraudulent websites and scams to get you to part with your money. People are increasingly cautious about the safety aspects of the web and as mentioned previously, one must assume that trust is automatically a barrier that you need to overcome. There are steps you might consider helping tackle this barrier. For instance, on your website you might publish details of your data protection registration, any trade body memberships, your registered company details etc. all of which create an air of transparency and build that feeling that the customer is dealing with a bona fide organisation. Even if you are not in control of your company website, but you are using social media, a similar approach can be taken. Share the good news, award nominations, customer testimonials, as these build trust and security for customers who see others are purchasing and you are being recognised by trustworthy parties.

In our case, we publish details of awards on our site, including those where we have been finalists, as it builds trust. Seeing an award from a recognised body demonstrates an endorsement that carries weight. The fact that you are even in the running for an award is a testament to your organisation, compared with its peers – so it can be useful even if you are not the outright winner.

Material On The Web

If you are producing material that will be on the Internet, you also need to have half an eye on the way that this will be viewed and served up to other prospective customers by search engines. The search engines, such as Google, are the indexes of the Internet that allow people to find information. Even if you have posted on social media, say a response to a customer question, it may still be possible to find that post via a search engine if it is properly constructed and optimised. This means that other customers, with similar needs, may come across your material and could enter your sales pipeline.

Optimising your content for the benefit of the search engines is a huge topic on its own, and one that would easily fill several more books!

Checkpoint Summary

1) Structure all communications with three parts in mind: Attract, Engage and Connect.

2) Attract – catch their eye with your opening.

3) Engage – deepen the connection with valuable content.

4) Connect – include a simple "call to action" that connects them with you.

A Distillation Of Our Sales System

So, this is our summary, but instead of restating everything that you have already read, I wanted to boil it all down into a simple system that you can follow – even if you have skipped straight to the back of the book. I find that in every book, or training course, there are a handful of useful tips that can be gleaned from the content. So here they are, ready distilled for you.

The first big point is to acknowledge that as times change it can become harder to rely exclusively upon sales techniques such as relationship building. Your repertoire can be expanded to encompass a broader understanding of how the process of helping a customer make a purchase works.

The Tipping Point Sales Balance & Adjustments

We like to see it as a balance along which there are various weights arranged, the weights being all the factors that are either barriers to a sale or contributors that motivate the customer to make a purchase. These weights can be moved. We call the movements "adjustments". The objective is to make adjustments that will bring the balance to its tipping point, where the contributors outweigh the barriers, and the customer purchases.

Not all sales will be winnable. Some are unwinnable and there are others that may be won according to the level of your Persuasion Proficiency. This is the level of skill with which you can adjust the sales balance.

This was the simple flow diagram that summarised the Tipping Point Sales System and our approach to identifying the forces that are at work and adjusting reach the point at which the sale is made:

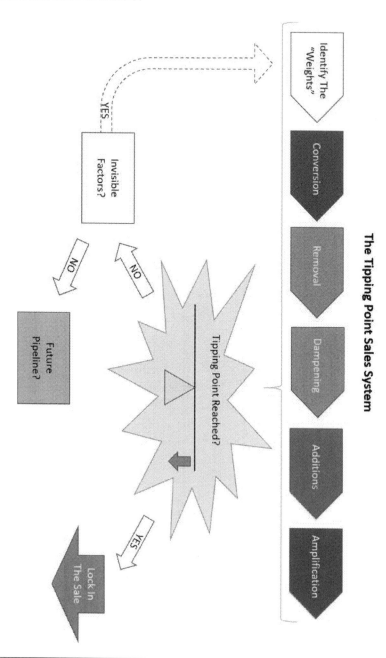

The Most Influential Weights

In any sales situation sense check your approach to ensure that you are making the best use of the most influential weights that you can apply to the balance. There may be a single weight that will result in a "slam dunk" outcome – look for that first.

If there is no single weight that stands out look for those that are most likely to have the greatest impact. These are likely to be those that are based on short supply or endorsement and following the crowd. These can have a powerful action on the customer's decision making and so are most likely to help you achieve tipping point.

Once the sales balance reaches the tipping point, lock in the decision in a way that demonstrates an obligation being placed upon your customer. That way they will be more reluctant to change their mind.

How To Best Use The Available Communication Channels

In addition to using this simple system, you should try and make use of the communication channels that are available to you, for example, keeping in contact with prospects using an email update.

Whatever methods you are using for your communication, remember to think about the three parts of each communication:

Attract (the headline to grab the customer) – Engage (more detail) – Connect (the call to action).

Finally

So, there you have it, our simple sales system - into which all techniques fit, and through which you can develop your Persuasion Proficiency. In turn, that will lead to an improvement in your sales conversion. You no longer need worry about which technique from your toolkit is going to be best, you simply follow the Tipping Point Sales System, which maximises your success rate automatically.

Notes

<hr>

ⁱ *What Glenn doesn't say is he interviewed me for the job with that high street bank!*

ⁱⁱ *In a recent seminar on closing techniques that I ran for a team of Customer Managers (not front-line sales) one delegate was role-playing as a salesperson with a colleague as a customer. She was delighted to feedback a common victory cry to the rest of the group: "I got him to sign on the dotted line". To which her "customer" responded "I didn't actually sign anything, but I said I would go ahead and we shook hands on it".*

ⁱⁱⁱ *A good example of how to appeal to the tactile customer is found in the rise of Apps, like the augmented reality versions that customise your choice, offered by the car industry. If your customer service proposition includes an app or online log in, make sure you have a version that the customer can explore – don't restrict yourself with a demonstration film. Whilst all types will love to see how it works, the tactile customer will love to find out for themselves.*

^{iv} *When working in a highly competitive relationship-centred financial services environment, I managed salespeople at both ends of the spectrum. A salesperson, let's call him Bob, had the longest pipeline of any in my team. In weekly meetings he was irrepressibly optimistic about the prospect of each one. Nothing ever died a natural death and whenever a prospect was lost to a competitor, it was also a total surprise. Even though the average time from lead to client was 90 days, Bob's zombie army just kept on tottering around.*

We worked on his closing techniques and I discovered Bob was a nice guy who was embarrassed to ask directly for the business.

Another sales guy: "Steve" was the opposite. He had almost nothing "in transit" because he evaluated his proposals and sought to close them quickly. The trouble was, his evaluation was often at odds with our credit policy and he missed the diamonds in the rough.

This book should help you find the successful medium between Bob and Steve.

ᵛ There are deposit savings clubs whereby everyone saves a set amount and one person is selected, at random, to get the full amount of their deposit each month. You may get your full deposit in month 1, when you have only saved a fraction of the total, but you may also have to wait until the final month.

ᵛⁱ *Right after I presented this exact strategy to a client in my training business whose customer list was literally world-class, I had an email from a delegate saying he did as I suggested and won a tender for a new monthly retainer on a marketing consultancy at a cost 60% higher than a competitor had quoted. The very next day after my workshop he met with his customer's head of finance to run through the tender. He stuck to the script and won.... I should have doubled their fee!*

[vii] I saw a fantastic example of using short supply and safety in numbers recently, on the website of a major online retailer. As you view particular items, a banner flashes up stating the number of people that are viewing this particular item at the moment. This reassures you that other people are buying the same thing, and at the same time it plants a seed of concern that the item could soon be in short supply or even sell out – increasing the motivation to purchase. A few seconds later, a second banner states the number of people that have purchased the item within the last 24 hours. Again, this reinforces those same feelings that there is safety in numbers, others have already purchased, and that the item may soon be out of stock.

[viii] *And be careful because sometimes it absolutely does NOT fit all. Humans want first to stand out from the crowd so as to attract a mate, and then to fit in, to belong to a large group, because of safety in numbers. So, depending on your product, recognise that some people want to hear, see and touch exclusivity, secret prices, just-for-you products or deals, limited editions, rare experiences or one offs. They are not ready to go where others have been because they want to stand out. It's a subconscious desire to be different and hence to be attractive in the sense of raising the attention of potential suitors. You need to listen to their needs first before you apply the weights that say "loads of my customers have bought this product" as that's a different proposition.*

[ix] *If you are struggling with this, or if you don't agree it, think about how people and sell and why we buy insurance. "We never know what's round the corner" said the recent ad for a major insurance comparison site. There is no certainty in insurance. If there were, either you wouldn't be able to buy a policy (as no-one would provide cover for something they knew they would have to pay a claim on), or you wouldn't want to (because it's never going to happen, so you don't need it). But insurance helps you bet against probability. Your premium is a risk you are willing to take to have the "certainty" of protection.*

Remember earlier when we mentioned "satisficing"? The tendency of entrepreneurs to accept the first practical solution they come across? This is surely a reaction informed by loss aversion. Remember not to be too negative when you use it.

[x] *It's an actual pleasure to hear a sales person add their "do you want it or don't you" weight to the scales with just enough urgency and even a sense of frustration, but not let it move over into petulance or even anger. If you think you need to bully, shame or embarrass the customer into buying from you, my advice is to re-read this book!*

[xi] *In my training workshops and seminars this is always voted as the best technique to move the deal forward, particularly by those who sometimes do not want to appear pushy but more empathic. In the follow up sessions where I check which have worked, this one regularly comes top of the pile. Try it on your very next call.*

[xii] *When I workshop this closing technique, almost every delegate cringes at the thought of saying "I like you" to a customer, let alone writing it. So, use the more acceptable suggestions in the section.*

xiii *If you want to see this in action, visit some of the large car showroom companies. You can look at as many cars you want but you can only test drive one, maybe two. You cannot haggle the price on the windscreen, so don't try. At some point the salesperson will have approached you to see if you are serious about buying, or just kicking the tyres. They will leave you if it's the latter. If you express and interest they will quickly determine your finance options, your choice, your deposit, your trade-in vehicle and maybe let you test drive, but usually after they have asked you "Are you going to buy this car today?" Should you offer any equivocation, they will answer your objections "I can't alter the price, perhaps there's a model with lower spec? If I find it, do you want it or don't you?" Then comes the part that would make a less determined salesperson blanche: if you say no, they excuse themselves and walk away to their next customer. You would have to call them back, or walk after them to catch them up, though I am told they are trained to walk slowly enough for this to happen!*

xiv I recall one of my relatives telling me that he hadn't committed to a particular purchase, despite signing the contract, as he had 14 days to pull out. I knew, as I suspect did the salesperson that got his signature on the order, that once the contract has been signed our desire to maintain direction kicks in, and we become much less likely to cancel.

Printed in Great Britain
by Amazon

48185950R00093